GM Marine Diesel

Lister-Petter Series AC1W Dieselite Marine Engine

Operating and Workshop Manual

GM Marine Diesel

Lister-Petter Series AC1W Dieselite Marine Engine

Operating and Workshop Manual

ISBN/EAN: 9783954274284
Erscheinungsjahr: 2014
Erscheinungsort: Bremen, Deutschland

© maritimepress in Europäischer Hochschulverlag GmbH & Co. KG, Fahrenheitstr. 1, 28359 Bremen. Alle Rechte beim Verlag und bei den jeweiligen Lizenzgebern.

www.maritimepress.de | office@maritimepress.de

Bei diesem Titel handelt es sich um den Nachdruck eines historischen, lange vergriffenen Buches. Da elektronische Druckvorlagen für diese Titel nicht existieren, musste auf alte Vorlagen zurückgegriffen werden. Hieraus zwangsläufig resultierende Qualitätsverluste bitten wir zu entschuldigen.

GM Marine Diesel

Lister-Petter Series AC1W Dieselite Marine Engine

Operating and Workshop Manual

OPERATING INSTRUCTIONS

Marine
DIESELITE
Series AC1W

WARNING

GENERATING SETS WHICH ARE EXPECTED TO RUN ON LOADS OF 50% OR BELOW MUST BE *RUN IN ON FULL LOAD* FOR AN INITIAL PERIOD OF 6 HRS. AND SUBSEQUENTLY FOR 2 HRS. EVERY 100 HRS. OF OPERATION, AT THE MAX. POWER THAT CAN BE TAKEN FROM THE UNIT.

FAILURE TO CARRY OUT THIS PROCEDURE MAY RESULT IN GLAZING OF THE BORES GIVING RISE TO EXCESSIVE EXHAUST EMISSION, GREATER OIL CONSUMPTION, LOSS OF POWER AND EVENTUAL SHORTENING OF THE ENGINE LIFE.

On receipt of plant, user should insert details from plant data plate to table on this page.

This will ensure that when any request for assistance is made the plan details are readily available.

MARINE DIESELITE

IMPORTANT WHEN ORDERING PARTS ALWAYS QUOTE		
MODEL NO:	SPEC:	
SERIAL NO:		
A.C. VOLTS	PHASE	HZ
MAX. RATING KVA	KW	pF
CONT. RATING KVA	KW	AMPS
BATT. VOLTS	AMPS	WATTS
R.P.M.	GEN. NO.	
CONTRACT NO:		

INSTRUCTIONAL AND SPARE PARTS MANUAL
FOR
MARINE DIESELITE AC1W SERIES
G & M PUBLICATION 475 GM 327

SECTION A	INTRODUCTION
SECTION B	INSTALLATION AND TECHNICAL DESCRIPTIONS
SECTION C	OPERATION AND SERVICING
SECTION D	ENGINE OVERHAUL
SECTION E	SPARE PARTS LISTS
SECTION F	A.C. GENERATOR TYPE LC.
SECTION G	A.C. GENERATOR TYPE RN.4050
SECTION H	**A.C. GENERATOR TYPE SC21**

SECTION A
INTRODUCTION

A1	THE FLYWEIGHT MARINE DIESELITE
A2	POST DELIVERY CHECK
A3	PLANT TECHNICAL DATA
A4	PLANT PHOTOGRAPHS
A5	APPROVED LUBRICANTS
A6	ALTERNATOR TYPES

A1–1 THE FLYWEIGHT MARINE DIESELITE

The G & M Power Plant Flyweight Marine Dieselite is a compact and robust power unit specially suited for use in small marine craft and introduces a much advanced and relaxed standard of living afloat.

The power available allows the use of a small electric cooker, domestic electrical appliances, heating, lighting, radio, etc. in combinations not exceeding the rating stamped on the plant data plate.

To obtain the long and reliable service of which the plant is capable this instruction book has been compiled to assist owners and users to carry out the periodical attentions necessary to maintain the plant in top condition.

A2–1 POST DELIVERY CHECK

Immediately the plant is received an examination should be carried out for transit damage and if damage has occurred the carrier must be informed.

Before dispatch from the G & M P.P. Works every plant has been subjected to a programme of mechanical and electrical performance testing, all adjustments have been set to give the correct rated output, and no alteration to any setting is necessary under normal atmospheric conditions to put the plant into service.

The lubricating oil has been drained and no attempt to start the plant must be made until the oil sump has been filled to its correct capacity.

The fuel system and cylinder head combustion chamber have been inhibited, and in order that the inhibiter protective film is not disturbed, the engine should not be turned until ready for starting. Engines treated with corrosion inhibitor do not require any special de-inhibiting treatment before starting.

A3–1 PLANT DATA

Model	Max Rating BS649			
	0.8PF	U.P.F.	VOLTS	HERTZ
4AC1W–52R	4.0	3.2	230	50
4AC1W–52SC	4.0	3.2	120/240	50
405 AC1W–63R	4.5	3.6	120/240	60

Dimensions and weights are approximate

LENGTH 'A'		WIDTH		HEIGHT 'B'		WEIGHT	
in.	mm.	in.	mm.	in.	mm.	lb.	kg.
30	762	17	432	20	508	240	109

Cooling: By direct sea water pump.

Combustion: Indirect injection. LANOVA combustion system.

Fuel System: By mechanical fuel lift pump. Fuel: Diesel B.S. 2869 Class A1 or A2. Consumption approx. 0.45 lb/B.H.P./HR. at 3000 rev/min.

Air Cleaner: Heavy duty replaceable paper element.

Governor: Centrifugal type incorporated within crankcase, maintains pre-set speed constant within B.S. 649

Lubrication: Pressure fed by rotary pump through to big end and main bearings. Small end bearing and camshaft are splash-lubricated. Replaceable oil filter housed in the crankcase. Sump capacity 4¾ pts. (2.7 litres). Oil consumption at full load 0.035 pts./HR. (19.9 ml/HR.)

Derating: For temperature: 2% per 5½°C. (10°F.) above 30°C. (85°F).

Self starting A.C. Models: Electrical start by 12v. automotive-type starter motor. Generator exciter field provides trickle charge (max. 150 watts) to starter battery.

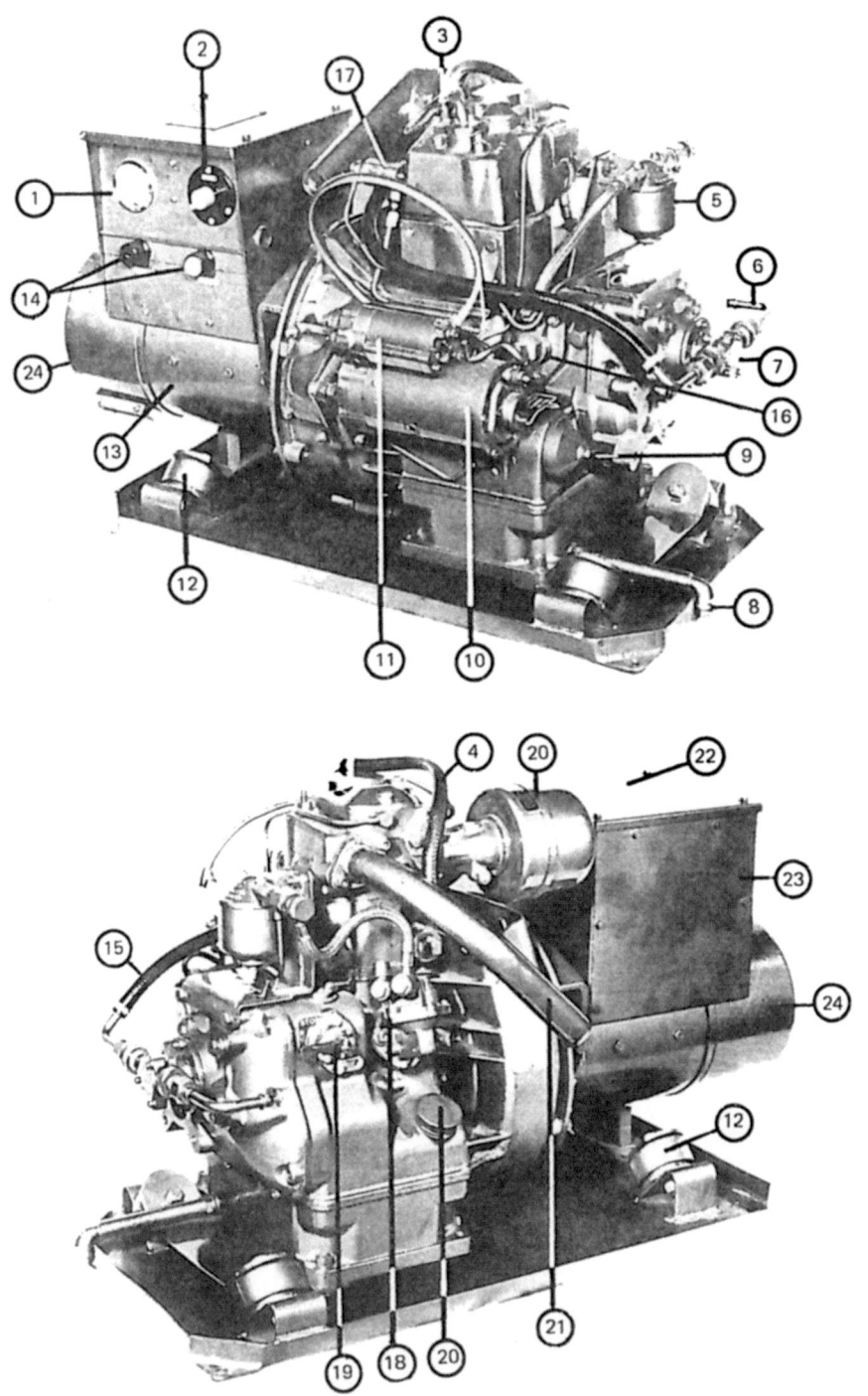

A4-1 PLANT PHOTOGRAPHS

A4—1 KEY TO PHOTOGRAPHS
1. CHARGE AMMETER
2. START BUTTON
3. PRIMING PLUNGER
4. COOLING WATER OUTLET PIPE
5. FUEL FILTER
6. COOLING WATER INLET CONNECTION
7. WATER PUMP
8. OIL DRAIN EXTENSION
9. OIL FILTER
10. STARTER MOTOR
11. STARTER SOLENOID
12. ANTI VIBRATION MOUNTS
13. GENERATOR
14. BATTERY TERMINALS
15. COOLING WATER HOSE. PUMP TO ENGINE
16. FUEL INJECTION PUMP
17. FUEL INJECTOR
18. FUEL LIFT PUMP
19. STOP RUN LEVER
20. AIR CLEANER
21. WATER INJECTION ELBOW
22. DATA PLATE
23. CONTROL BOX
24. GENERATOR END COVER

NOTE. The location of the components indicated in the photographs will in general apply to all AC1W models, but design changes resulting from continuous development may produce small deviations from the model shown.

A5—1 APPROVED LUBRICANTS

The engine oils listed under approved lubricants are heavy duty oils with a minimum detergency as specified by British Defence Specification No. 2101D or U.S. Specification MIL/L/2104B. Suitable additional heavy duty oils will be recommended by a local oil distributor, but a minimum detergency as above must be specified.

Supplier	U.K. Winter & Summer Up to 30°C (86°F)	Tropical Above 30°C (86°F)
Shell Group of Companies	Rotella SX Oil lOW Rotella TX Oil lOW Rotella TX Oil lOW/30 X-100 lOW Talona Oil lOW	Rotella SX Oil 20/20W Rotella TX Oil 20/20W Rotella SX Oil 20W/40 Rotella TX Oil 20W/40 Super Oil Tractor Oil Universal
Mobil Oil Co. Ltd	Delvac Special 10/30 Delvac 1210	Delvac Special lOW/30 Mobiloil Special lOW/30 Mobiland Universal lOW/30 Mobiloil 20W/30 Delvac 1220 Mobilgard 212
B.P. Companies	Vanellus lOW Super Visco-Static lOW/40	Vanellus 20W Vanellus 20W/30 Super Visco-Static 20W/50 Energol IC-M20W Tractor Oil Universal 20W/30

Castrol Ltd.	Deusol CRI 10 Deusol CRB 10 Deusol CRB 10W/30 Castrol CRI 10 Castrol CRB 10 Agricastrol Multi-Use 10W/30	Deusol CRI 20 Deusol CRB 20 Deusol CRB 10W/30 Deusol CRM Castrol CRB 20 Castrol 210 MX Agricastrol Multi-Use 20W/30
Esso Petroleum Co. Ltd.	Essolube HD 10W Essolube HDX 10W Essolube D-3 HP 10W Essolube D-3 10W Essolube HDX 10W/30 Esso Motor Oil 10W	Essolube HD 20W Essolube HDX 20W Essolube D-3 HP 10W Essolube D-3 10W Essolube HDX 10W/30 Esso Motor Oil 20W
Caltex (U.K.) Ltd.	Supreme Five Star Motor Oil 10W/30 Custom Five Star Motor Oil 10W/30 Five Star Motor Oil 10W RPM Delo 200 Oil 10W/30 RPM Delo 200 Oil 10W RPM Delo 100 Oil 10W	Supreme Five Star Motor Oil 10W/30 Custom Five Star Motor Oil 10W/30 Five Star Motor Oil 20/20W RPM Delo 200 Oil 10W/30 RPM Delo 200 Oil 20/20W RPM Delo 100 Oil 20/20W
Chevron Oil Co. Ltd.	Chevron Delo Special Motor Oil 10W Chevron Delo 200 Motor Oil 10W	Chevron Delo Special Motor Oil 20/20W Chevron Delo 200 Motor Oil 20/20W
Texaco Ltd.	Ursa Extra Duty 10W Ursa Extra Duty 10W/30 Havoline Motor Oil 10W Havoline Motor Oil 10W/40	Ursa Extra Duty 20W Ursa Extra Duty 10W/30 Havoline Motor Oil 20/20W Havoline Motor Oil 10W/40
Gulf Oil (G.B.) Ltd.	Gulflube Motor Oil XHD 10W Gulflube Motor Oil XHD 10W/30 Gulf Multi-G 10W/30	Gulflube Motor Oil XHD 20/20W Gulflube Motor Oil XHD 10W/30 Gulf Multi-G 10W/30 Gulf Superfleet 20W/30

NOTE: Since some SAE 10W oils are thinner than SAE 10W/30 multigrades at low temperatures, the starting of the engine at these temperatures will be marginally better using SAE 10W oils.

A6-1 ALTERNATOR TYPES

Three different types of alternator are currently used on the AC1W Series of generating sets:— LC, RN4050 and SC21. The types of alternator fitted can be identified by reference to the GEN. NO. column on the Data Plate.

SECTION B

INSTALLATION AND TECHNICAL DESCRIPTIONS

- **B1** INSTALLATION GENERAL
- **B2** POSITIONING AND ATTACHMENT
- **B3** VENTILATION
- **B4** FUEL SYSTEM
- **B5** LUBRICATION
- **B6** COOLING SYSTEM
- **B7** EXHAUST SYSTEM
- **B8** REMOTE STARTING

B1–1 INSTALLATION GENERAL

It is not possible to provide a set of detailed instructions which will apply equally to all installations, but the essential requirements necessary for the reliable and satisfactory performance of the plant must be inherent features of all installation designs and layouts.

It is recommended that before commencing the installation the technical information in Sections A & B of this publication be read, the requirements of each individual system noted and the installation carried out as an integrated project in which the needs of each system are satisfied.

The maximum of angle of installation including bow lift is $12°$ and thwartships is $22°$

B2–1 POSITIONING AND ATTACHMENT

Rope slings passing underneath the engine and generator may be used with suitable lifting equipment to raise the plant and place it in position.

The plant must not be positioned with the end of the generator so close to a bulkhead that the cooling air flow through the generator is restricted and overheating occurs.

Allow sufficient space around the plant for periodic servicing to be carried out and to ensure easy access for the more frequent requirements of fuel and oil contents checking and replenishment.

The plant must be mounted on a firm structure or decking which must be of sufficient mass to enable engine vibration to be absorbed by the flexible mounts. The bed must be of adequate strength to ensure security at all times, and under all sea conditions.

B3–1 VENTILATION

The installation compartment must be provided with air inlet and outlet ducts which will allow a continuous flow of cool air through the compartment when the vessel is both under way and stationary. The quantity of air must be sufficient for engine combustion and generator cooling, air already heated must not be allowed to recirculate.

When the plant is installed in an existing engine room the ventilation system must be capable of catering for the generating set as well as the main engines.

B4–1 FUEL SYSTEM

Diesel engines must have clean fuel, cleanliness and care are especially important when the system is installed, dirt left in the fuel tank or fuel lines will lead to fuel feed troubles. Water contamination of fuel is a frequent source of trouble in boats, especially sea water, as the highly corrosive action of salt water will cause serious damage to the fuel system components.

Galvanised steel must not be used for any part of the fuel system, diesel fuel attacks the plating which flakes and causes blockages in the fuel system; all rubber hoses used must be resistant to diesel fuel.

It is normal practice to take the fuel supply from the vessels main fuel tank, but if a separate tank is preferred a capacity of 10 galls. (45 litres) will normally be sufficient subject to daily replenishment. When the tank is situated below the level of the engine, the vertical distance between the fuel level and the fuel lift pump must not exceed the maximum lift of the fuel pump which is 2' (610 mm.)

Fuel tanks must be secure under all sea conditions provide easy access for refuelling and be electrically earthed. Large capacity tanks should have internal baffles.

The underside of the fuel tank should incorporate a well in which any accumulation of water can be drained, and the top of the tank be vented to atmosphere.

The suction end of the fuel supply pipe must be slightly clear of the bottom of the tank, and an ON/OFF supply cock fitted at the tank. A sedimenter positioned in the supply line between the tank and the engine must form the lowest point of the fuel system.

The connection of the fuel supply to the fuel lift pump on the engine should be made with a section of flexible fuel pipe to allow for engine movement on its flexible mounts. The engine recirculates its own excess fuel and no spill return to the tank is necessary. A hand priming lever on the fuel pump is provided for filling and venting the fuel system, which is a required procedure when the engine is started for the first time and when ever the fuel system is disturbed.

B4–2 SAFETY NOTE

Do not use plastic hose for flexible fuel lines.

Do not use direct reading sight glass forms of fuel contents guages

B4-3 FUEL

The fuel used should be high grade light diesel fuel, gas oil or derv fuel. It should comply with B.S. 2869: 1967 Class A1 or A2. Winter and summer grades of diesel fuels are marketed during the appropriate seasons and are also graded for that part of the world in which they are intended to be used. Diesel fuels available for use in low temperature climates are classified as "cold reference fuels" Make sure the fuel being used is suitable for the prevailing temperature conditions.

Some diesel fuels not suitable for low temperatures may form wax under these conditions. If it is suspected that wax has formed, the whole engine should be gently warmed through, and the fuel tank, pipes, injector and fuel then completely drained and flushed with the correct fuel. Refill the fuel system with correct fuel and bleed and prime before attempting to start.

B4-4 TO BLEED THE FUEL SYSTEM Fig. 1B

(a) Turn on the fuel supply.
(b) Ensure that the fuel solenoid is energised and the Stop/Run lever (A) is against the roll pin limit stop.
(c) Loosen the two vent screws (B) on the top of the filter and operate the fuel lift pump until bubble free fuel leaks from the vent screws. Tighten the vent screws.
(d) Loosen the vent screw (C) if fitted on the fuel injection pump and operate the fuel lift pump until bubble free fuel leaks from the vent screw. Tighten the vent screw on the injection pump.
(e) Lift and hold the decompression lever (D) in the vertical position and turn the engine on the starter motor approximately 15 revolutions and listen for the squeak of the injector.

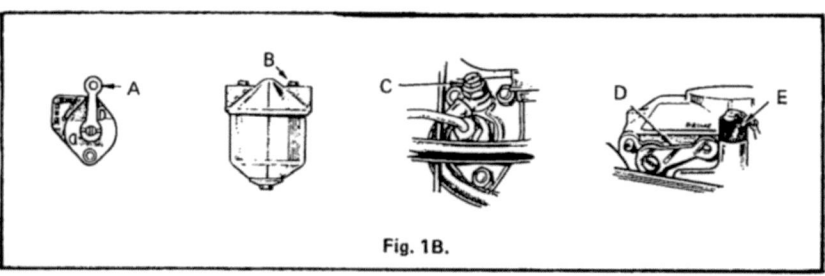

Fig. 1B.

B5-1 LUBRICATION

The capacity of the oil sump is 4¾ pints (2.7 litres) and the level mark on the dipstick should be checked daily before starting.

A sump drain pump is fitted to the engine to facilitate ease of oil draining.

A protection device is incorporated which will automatically stop the engine, if, due to lack of oil or for any other reason the normal oil pressure of 35 lbf/in^2 (2.46 kgf/cm^2) falls to 15 lbf/in^2 (1.05 kgf/cm^2). See Section C1-6.

B6-1 COOLING SYSTEM

Sea water is used for cooling which after leaving the cylinder head is injected into the exhaust system for overboard discharge.

It is important that to avoid corrosion by galvanic action between dissimilar metals that brass or copper pipes or fittings are kept to a minimum and under no circumstances placed in direct contact with the aluminium of the engine.

The sea water intake should comprise a sea cock and strainer with a $\frac{3}{8}$" (9.5mm) bore inboard connection, and $\frac{3}{8}$" bore rubber hose for piping cooling water to and from the engine.

The sea inlet must be positioned below the water line and not become exposed and draw in air when the boat heels. The vertical distance between the water line and the sea water pump must not exceed the maximum water lift of the pump which is 2' (610 mm.)

Forward facing inlet scoops should not be used as the forward velocity of the vessel may create sufficient ram pressure to drive water past the pump impeller and into the engine when it is not running.

Before starting the plant for the first time the cooling water supply should be turned off and the pump impeller examined to ensure that it is not sticking to the pump body. Lightly lubricate the impeller with petroleum jelly.

The impeller should be examined at regular intervals of three months under normal conditions and more frequently when operating in silted waters.

After any servicing or repairs to the pump, ensure the cooling water supply is turned on before starting the engine, and immediately after the engine has started check that the cooling water is being injected into the exhaust system.

As a protection against salt water corrosion attacking the internal surfaces of the cooling water jacket an inhibiter plug is fitted. When in contact with salt water the inhibiter plug readily corrodes leaving the surrounding materials unaffected. The plug should be examined every three months and renewed when deterioration of 50% or more has occurred. When correctly fitted the plug should be screwed in until it butts internally and the screwdriver end is flush with the outisde of the cylinder head. To assist in water sealing the threads of the plug should be wrapped in P.T.F.E. tape.

The plug is illustrated in the cylinder head spare parts list item No. WAB. 275a.

NOTE: On later engines the inhibiter plug is situated in the cooling water entry adaptor at the base of the cylinder.

It is recommended that the cooling system be drained in cold weather and also before allowing the engine to stand idle.

A protection device is incorporated which will automatically stop the engine if the water temperature rises above 75°C (167°F).

B7–1 EXHAUST SYSTEM Fig. 2B

Wet exhaust systems for marine installations must efficiently discharge the waste combustion gases to atmosphere and effectively prevent any back flow of water in the system flooding the engine.

Bends in the system must be kept to a minimum and made as wide as possible, acute bends which slow down the flow of escaping gases, increase the exhaust back pressure with subsequent overheating and loss of engine efficiency must be avoided.

To prevent any back flow of water in the system reaching the engine, a section of pipe in the form of a "Swan neck" must be fitted to form the highest point of the system with the final section of the exhaust run inclining downward to the overboard discharge point.

When plants are installed below the water line it is possible when the vessel is either under way or stationary and the engine stopped, for the sea water to seep through the pump by syphoning action. If this should happen the water may fill the exhaust system and eventually enter the engine through an open exhaust valve and thence into the air induction system through an open inlet valve and flood the compartment.

To prevent syphoning occurring a syphon break must be fitted. This requires that the water outlet hose from the cylinder to the water injection elbow be raised to form an inverted "U" at least 12" above the water line. See Fig. 2B. The inverted "U" pipe must incorporate a vacuum relief valve which under normal operating conditions will be closed. If after the engine has stopped and a pressure drop occurs within the "U" pipe, the relief valve will open to equalise the pressure so that syphoning cannot take place.

B7–2 WATERLIFT EXHAUST MUFFLER

For extremely quiet running, it is recommended that a G & M Waterlift Silencer is used.

The Waterlift system cools the hot exhaust gases muffles the exhaust noise and using the Kinetec energy of the exhaust gases, lifts the cooling liquid to a height of four feet for convenient discharge above the waterline.

The muffler should be located on a sturdy base slightly below the engine exhaust level. Fig. 2B illustrates an exhaust layout for below the waterline installations and shows a syphon break and a Waterlift Silencer.

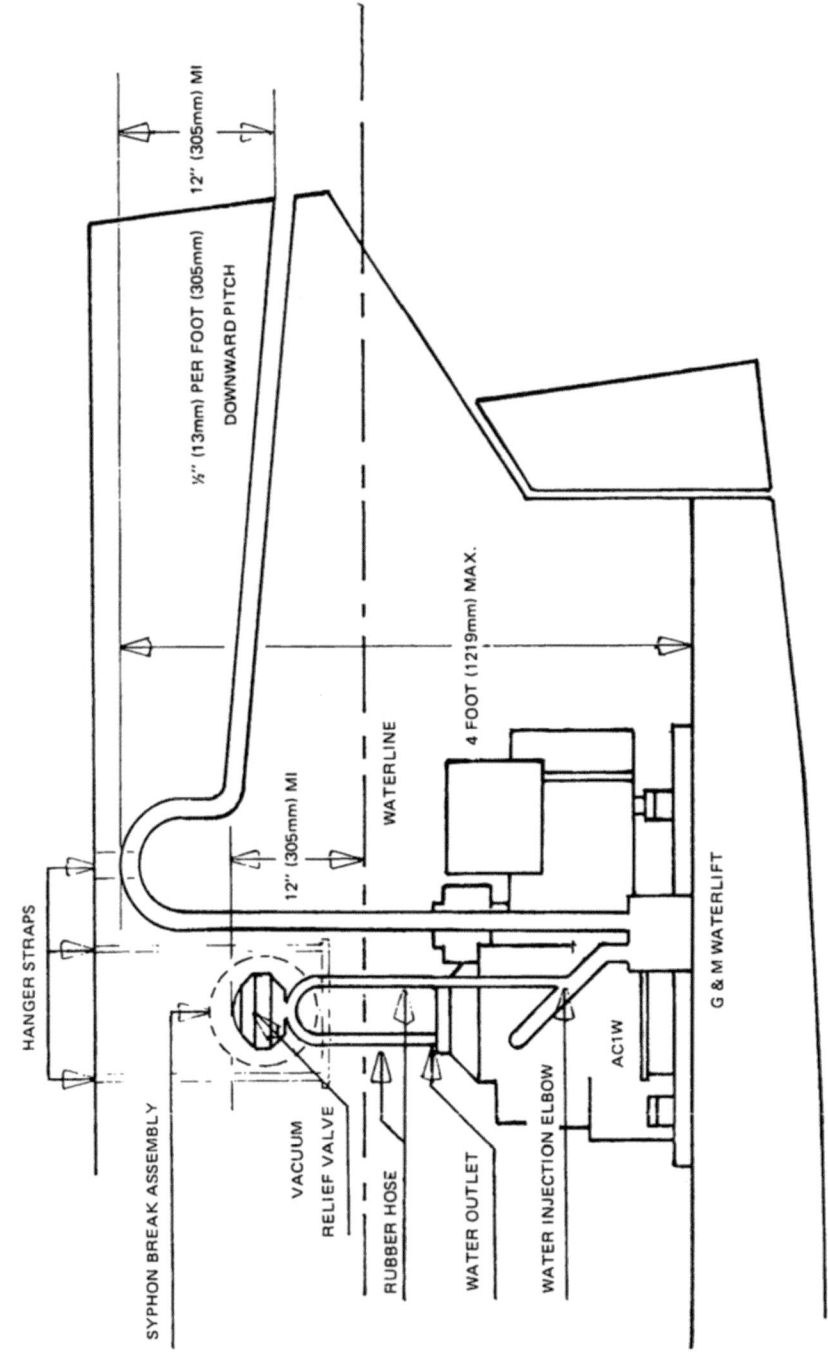

Fig. 2B
G & M Waterlift Exhaust muffler below waterline installation using Syphon Break

B7–3 EXHAUST BACK PRESSURE Fig. 3B

The maximum exhaust back pressure for the AC1W engine is given as 6" water gauge. This can be measured using a transparent plastic hose partly filled with water, one end of the hose being connected to a straight section of the exhaust as near to the engine as possible, and the other end open to atmosphere.

With the engine running on full load measure the distance between the two water levels which must not exceed 6" (152 mm) equal to .216 1bf/in^2.

B8–1 REMOTE STARTING FACILITY

A seven way terminal block in the control box is provided for wiring in duplicate controls for remote operation.

The components are supplied loose as individual items for fitment as desired, either in the wheelhouse console or an electrical panel.

The items consist of:—

Key switch (identical with control box switch)	Qty. 1
AC indicator light (neon)	Qty. 1
DC Warning lamp	Qty. 1

The cable length between the plant and the remote controls should not exceed 30ft.(9.5 metres) using cable with a cross sectional area of not less than 4.040 mm.

If the cable length is required to be more than 30 ft., a heavier cable must be used to ensure that voltage at the starter motor does not drop below 10 volts during cranking.

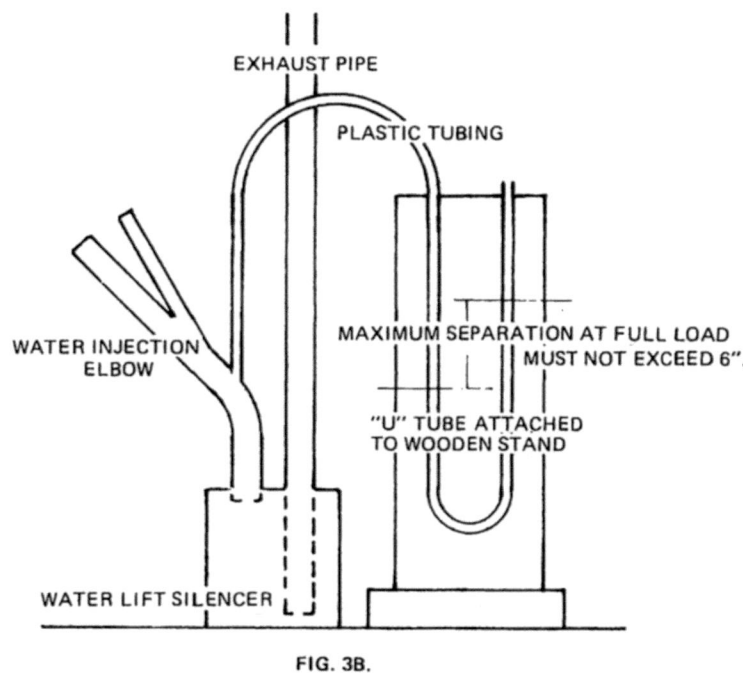

FIG. 3B.

NOTE:— To check the exhaust back pressure, it is necessary as a temporary fitment only, that an adaptor for the plastic tubing be placed in the exhaust run between the water injection elbow and the water lift silencer.

SECTION C

OPERATION AND SERVICING

C1 STARTING AND STOPPING
C2 SPECIAL OPERATING INSTRUCTIONS
C3 PERIODIC SERVICING
C4 PRESERVATION

C1 STARTING AND STOPPING

C1–1 STARTING THE PLANT FOR THE FIRST TIME
(a) Fill the oil sump to the high level mark on the dipstick.
(b) Remove the front cover from the sea water pump and examine the impeller, ensure that it is not sticking to the pump body. If dry, lubricate with petroleum jelly. Replace the front cover.
(c) Turn on the cooling water supply.
(d) Turn on the fuel supply and bleed the fuel system (See B4–4).
(e) Turn and hold the start switch key in the "start" position until the engine fires then release the key to the "run" position. Immediately after the engine has started check that the cooling water is being injected into the exhaust system.
N.B. Do not operate the starter motor for more then 20 seconds at a time. Observe an interval of 10 seconds before making a second attempt to start.
(f) Check for signs of fuel, oil, or coolant leaks, apply electrical load progressively. After a few minutes remove the load and stop the engine. (See C1–5). Allow time for the oil to settle in the sump and then check the level on the dipstick.

C1–2 NORMAL START AT THE PLANT
(a) Ensure that the daily and pre-start checks have been carried out, all electrical loads isolated and the decompression lever is horizontal.
(b) Turn and hold the start switch key in the "start" position until the engine fires then release the key to the "run" position.
N.B. Do not operate the starter motor for more than 20 seconds at a time. Observe an interval of 10 seconds before making a second attempt to start.

C1–3 NORMAL START REMOTE
The pre-start checks and procedures for remote starting are the same as for starting at the plant with the following exceptions:–

From the remote position it may not be possible to hear the engine start, but a visual indication that the engine has started, and the plant is running, is provided when the DC failure warning light extinguishes and the AC Neon light illuminates.

C1–4 COLD STARTING
(a) Below 0°C (32°F) and if the engine is cold, it is essential to prime the engine for hand starting. Proceed as follows:
   (i) Remove the priming plunger (E). Fig. 1B
   (ii) Fill the priming chamber with engine oil – NOT fuel.
   (iii) Replace the priming plunger and press down.
   (iv) Repeat (i), (ii) and (iii) as above.
   (v) It is advisable to keep a quantity of lubricating oil in a suitable container for this purpose.
(b) Should the engine fire and then stop, prime again as above before attempting to start.
(c) If under cold conditions the engine does not run up to its rated speed after starting, operate the priming plunger again while the engine is running.
(d) To minimise cold starting difficulties, it is a wise policy to keep the engine under cover when not in use and to ensure that an SAE IOW viscosity engine oil is used (see Approved Lubricants).
(e) Below –9°C (16°F) consult: G & M P.P. or their agents for starting instructions.

C1–5 NORMAL STOP
(a) Remove electrical load and allow engine to run for 1 – 2 minutes on no load.
(b) Turn the key switch to the OFF position.

C1-6 AUTOMATIC EMERGENCY STOP

Low oil pressure or high water temperature will operate the contacts in the appropriate switch and complete a circuit to de-energise the fuel solenoid and stop the plant.

Under these conditions the key switch will still be in the "run" position, the fuel solenoid remaining energised, the electrical load still connected and the warning light illuminated.

Operators finding a plant stopped under these conditions must:
- (a) Turn the key switch to "OFF", de-energising the fuel solenoid and extinguishing the failure warning lamp.
- (b) Isolate the electrical load.
- (c) Investigate and rectify the cause of the shutdown before attempting to restart the plant.

C2-1 SPECIAL OPERATING INSTRUCTIONS
- (a) Do not stop the engine by means of the decompressor. This will lead to damaged valve seats and cylinder head joints.
- (b) Never allow the fuel tank to run dry and stop the engine, this will allow air into the fuel system.
- (c) Drain the cooling system if the engine has to be left idle during cold weather.
- (d) When operating in water with a high silt content the inspection of the water pump and the flushing through of the cooling system must be carried out at more frequent intervals than laid down in periodic servicing.
- (e) Always close the cooling water sea cock, before disconnecting any part of the cooling system.
- (f) Always close the fuel supply cock before disconnecting any part of the fuel system.

C3 PERIODIC SERVICING

C3-1 DAILY
- (a) Check fuel and oil levels — replenish as necessary.
- (b) Ensure that all cooling air apertures are unobstructed.

C3-2 PRE-START
- (a) Ensure that all electrical loads are isolated.
- (b) Check that there are no loose articles on the plant.
- (c) Check that the cooling water supply is turned on.

C3-3 WEEKLY
- (a) Check the level of the electrolyte in the starter battery.
- (b) Examine the battery terminals for corrosion, clean as necessary.

C3-4 SERVICE AFTER THE FIRST 20 HOURS

When the plant has completed 20 hours running it can be considered "run in" and the following items of service must be carried out:—
- (a) When the engine is hot, drain the oil sump, flush out with flushing oil, change the oil filter and refill with new oil.
- (b) Check the tightness of the cylinder head nuts. This must not be carried out when the engine is hot.
- (c) Check tappet clearances and adjust as necessary. (See D3—9)
- (d) Examine water pump impeller for damage.
- (e) Check all water hose joints for tightness.
- (f) Check all components for security of attachment.

C3-5 EVERY 3 MONTHS
Examine the corrosion inhibiter plug, fit a new plug if the deterioration is 50% or more.

C3-6 EVERY 100 HOURS
Drain the oil sump and refill with new oil.

Examine slip rings and brushes.

C3–7 EVERY 200 HOURS
   (a) Disconnect the starter battery.
   (b) Turn off the cooling water supply.
   (c) Turn off the fuel supply.
   (d) Check the tightness of the cylinder head nuts. Refer to the table of Torque Settings. (See Section D1–2). Do not tighten when the engine is hot.
   (e) Check the tappet clearances. Adjust as necessary.
   (f) Drain the oil sump, flush out with flushing oil, fit a new oil filter element and joint ring and refill the sump with new oil.
   (g) Clean the air filter by gently tapping on a solid surface to loosen dry dirt, or blow out with a pressure air jet.
   (h) Examine water pump impeller, clean the pump internally and lubricate the impeller with petroleum jelly.
   (j) Remove the A.C. generator enclosing cover, use an air pressure jet to blow out carbon dust and examine brushes and sliprings for damage and wear. Check brushes for freedom of movement in their holders. Renew worn or damaged brushes. Replace enclosing cover.
   (k) Reconnect starter battery.
   (l) Turn on fuel supply and cooling water supply.
   (m) Check all components for security of attachment.

C3–8 EVERY 400 HOURS
   (a) Fit new air cleaner element.
   (b) Flush out the cylinder and cylinder head cooling waterways with clean fresh water. Exami the cylinder head corrosion inhibiter plug and replace if deteriorated.
   (c) Clean the fuel sedimenter.

C3–9 EVERY 800 HOURS
   (a) Fit a new fuel filter element.
   (b) Fit a new cylinder head gasket.

C3–10 EVERY 2000 HOURS
   (a) Decarbonise.
   (b) Clean out piston oil return holes.
   (c) Check cylinder bore for wear.
   (d) Examine crankshaft bearings and renew if clearance is excessive.
   (e) Clean the oil pump strainer.
   (f) Remove the fuel injector and test spray.

N.B. It is recommended that the 2000 hour service is carried out by an authorised Service Agent.

C3–11 END OF SEASON SERVICE

If the plant is to be taken out of service for the winter, it is recommended that an "end of season service" be carried out and should consist of the following:
   (a) The 200 hours service.
   (b) Any 200, 800, or 2000 hour items which are due.
   (c) The protection and preservation servicing.

C4—1 PROTECTION AND PRESERVATION

(a) ENGINE

Intermittent use:

When not in regular use, engines should be run for a thirty minute period each week to lubricate internal parts and boil off any condensation that has formed. External unpainted parts should be wiped with an oil rag, and external controls etc., lubricated.

Preservation:

Engines remaining idle for more than a month may corrode, and as serious damage may result it is recommended that they be preserved as follows:

(i) Drain the sump, flush out with flushing oil and refill with the appropriate grade of lubricating oil which will provide internal protection. (Alternatively, a lubricating oil with preservative properties will be recommended by a local oil distributor).

(ii) Drain the fuel tank and filter and refill with approximately 1 pint (0.57 litres) of *Shell Fusus* oil or *Calibration Fluid C*. Bleed and prime the fuel system and run the engine on light load for five minutes. The fuel system is now adequately protected.

(iii) Close the inlet water sea cock. Drain and flush the cooling system, including the heat exchanger if fitted.

(iv) The air inlet and exhaust manifolds should be sealed against the ingress of moisture.

(v) Ensure that the anti-vibration mountings are free from fuel or lubricating oil.

(vi) Protected engines require no attention before use other than removing the sealing covers, adding fuel and filling the heat exchanger, if fitted, with clean fresh water or an anti-freeze mixture.

(b) BATTERY

Disconnect, remove and thoroughly clean off all traces of acid, dirt and corrosion. Lightly coat terminals and connectors with anti sulphuric grease. Top up electrolyte to correct level and maintain battery in fully charged condition, checking the electrolyte level every 4 weeks. Batteries should be stored in a cool dry atmosphere.

(c) GENERATOR

Carry out 200 hour generator servicing and seal up all cooling air inlet and outlet apertures.

SECTION D

ENGINE OVERHAUL

D1	TECHNICAL DATA AND TORQUE SETTINGS
D2	COOLING SYSTEM
D3	DECARBONISING AND VALVE SERVICE
D4	CYLINDER AND PISTON
D5	CONNECTING ROD
D6	FLYWHEEL
D7	CRANKSHAFT
D8	CAMSHAFT
D9	GOVERNOR
D10	LUBRICATION SYSTEM
D11	FUEL SYSTEM
D12	TO ADJUST SPEED CONTROL
D13	AIR CLEANER
D14	STARTER MOTOR
D15	FAULT LOCATION

D1–1 ENGINE TECHNICAL DATA

Bore (nominal)	3in. (76.2mm)
Stroke	2.625in. (66.68mm)
Power and Speed (B.S. continuous rating):	2.8 bhp at 1500 rev/min.
	3.3 bhp at 1800 rev/min.
	4.0 bhp at 2100 rev/min.
	5.0 bhp at 2500 rev/mi
	6.0 bhp at 3000 rev/min.
	6.5 bhp at 3600 rev/min.
Cubic capacity	18.5 in^3 (304 cm^3)
Compression ratio	17 to 1
Lubricating oil pressure (min.)	35 lbf/in^2 (2.46 kgf/cm^2)
Fuel injection release pressure	2350/2650 lbf/in^2 (165.2/186.3 kgf/cm^2)
Fuel injection timing (by spill):	
Variable speed	28° before TDC
Inlet valve opens	13° before TDC
Inlet valve closes	38° after BDC
Exhaust valve opens	38° before BDC
Exhaust valve closes	13° after TDC
Oil capacity	4¾ pints (2.7 litres)
Lubricating oil	See approved list
Fuel	A high grade light distillate diesel fuel in accordance with B.S. Specification No. 2869: 1967 Class A1 or A2.
'Run through' water per bhph	3 gal. (13.6 litres)
Starter motor battery	12 Volts 50 Ampere hour (min.) Negative earth.
Camshaft end float	0.003/0.010in. (0.08/0.25 mm)
Crankshaft end float (new)	0.005/0.017in. (0.13/0.43mm)
Crankshaft end float (not to exceed)	0.020in. (0.51mm)
Crankpin ovality (not to exceed)	0.0025in. (0.063mm)
Cylinder bore wear (not to exceed)	0.010in. (0.25mm)
Piston ring gap (new)	0.012/0.017in. (0.30/0.43mm)
Piston ring gap (not to exceed)	0.045in. (1.14mm)
Exhaust valve lift by decompressor (max.)	0.015in. (0.38mm)
Bumping clearance	0.022/0.026in. (0.56/0.166mm)
Valve rocker clearance (cold)	0.004in. (0.10mm)
Valve depth from cylinder head face (new)	0.039/0.057in. (0.99/1.45mm)
Main bearing clearance (new)	0.0008/0.0029in. (0.020/0.077mm)
Large end bearing clearance (new)	0.0010/0.0035in. (0.025/0.090mm)
Small end bush diameter (fitted)	0.8753/0.8757in. (22.233/22.243mm)
Cylinder reboring diameters:	
Standard	3.000/3.001in. (76.20/76.23mm)
Oversize:	
0.020in.	3.020/3.021in. (76.71/76.73mm)
0.030in.	3.030/3.031in. (76.96/76.99mm)
0.040in.	3.040/3.041in. (77.22/77.24mm)
Crankshaft regrinding diameters:	Main journal and crankpin
Standard	1.6250/1.6245in. (41.275/41.262mm)
Undersize:	
0.010in.	1.6150/1.6145in. (41.021/41.008mm)
0.020in.	1.6050/1.6045in. (40.767/40.754mm)
Lubricating oil pump:	
Rotor end clearance (new)	0.001/0.0025in. (0.025/0.064mm)
Rotor end clearance (not to exceed)	0.005in. (0.127mm)
Rotor form clearance (new)	0.002/0.005in. (0.051/0.127mm)
Rotor form clearance (not to exceed)	0.008in. (0.203mm)
Shaft/bore clearance (new)	0.0015/0.003in. (0.038/0.076mm)
Shaft/bore clearance (not to exceed)	0.005in. (0.127mm)
Rotor shaft diameter (new)	0.5918/0.5923in. (15.032/15.044mm)

D1-2 TORQUE SPANNER SETTINGS

	lbf ft	kgf m
Large end bolt	25	3.46
Cylinder head nut	20	2.77
Injector stud nut	13	1.80
Flywheel nut	155	21.43
Flywheel extension or gearwheel bolt	27	3.73
Lubricating oil pump screw	10	1.38
Lubricating oil filter centre bolt	10	1.38
Fuel pump delivery union body	15	2.07
Crankshaft and camshaft extension shaft screw	14	1.94
Crankshaft gearwheel retaining screw	27	3.73
Camshaft gearwheel retaining screw	27	3.73

D2-1 TO DRAIN COOLING SYSTEM
(a) Shut off the sea cock and remove the plugs from the cylinder. This will allow the cooling water to drain out of the cylinder and cylinder head.

(b) Remove the pump outlet pipe and drain the cooling water from the hose.

(c) When replacing the cylinder plugs, it is advisable to wrap 1½ turns of 'P.T.F.E.' tape round the threads. This will prevent the plugs sticking and corroding.

(d) IMPORTANT. When reassembled and before starting the engine, ensure that the sea cock is opened.

(e) As the water pump is self-priming, there is no need to prime the cooling system.

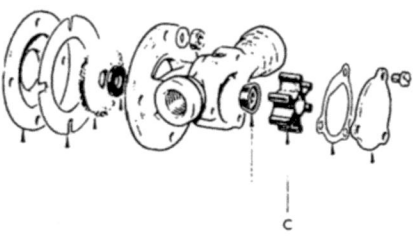

Fig. 1D

D2-2 TO FLUSH OUT CYLINDER AND CYLINDER HEAD
(a) Drain the cooling water from the cylinder and cylinder head.

(b) Disconnect the cooling water outlet hose, and remove the plug and pipe fittings from the cylinder head.

(c) By inserting a piece of wire through the various orifices in the cylinder and cylinder head, rake out any silt that has collected in the cooling system. This should be carried out while flushing with clean fresh water, preferably under pressure.

(d) It may be found necessary to flush the cooling system frequently when operating the engine in water with a high silt content.

(e) When replacing the plugs and pipe fittings, it is advisable to wrap 1½ turns of 'P.T.F.E.' tape round the threads. This will prevent the threads sticking and corroding.

D2-3 TO REMOVE WATER PUMP Fig. 1D
(a) Close the sea cock and remove the water pipes from the pump.

(b) Remove the attachment nuts and carefully slide the pump off the shaft.

(c) Remove the pump cover (A) and joint (B) and remove the impeller (C).

(d) Inspect the water sealing washer (D), water thrower (E), seal in the pump body (F) and the impeller for damage, and renew if necessary.

(e) It is not necessary to remove the cam plate from the inside of the pump body.

D2—4 TO REPLACE WATER PUMP Fig. 1D

(a) Replace the water pump adaptor (G) and shim (H), if removed. Replace the water sealing washer and water thrower, leaving a gap between them.

(b) Carefully slide the water pump body onto the shaft, with the cam plate screw uppermost and tighten up. Ensure that the water thrower is just clear of the pump body.

(c) Ensure that the pump shaft does not touch the pump cover when the water pump is replaced. If it does, extra shims must be added between the adaptor plate and the pump body.

(d) Replace the impeller on the shaft and refit joint and cover plate. The joint must be positioned so that the cam plate is covered.

(e) Replace the inlet and outlet pipes.

D3—1 DECARBONISING

A carbon deposit forms on piston and cylinder head and the presence of an excessive carbon deposit is usually indicated by a dirty exhaust and a falling off of power.

Decarbonising necessitates the removal of the cylinder head, followed by the removal of all carbon and the grinding in of the valves. These operations are described in subsequent paragraphs.

D3—2 TO REMOVE CYLINDER HEAD

(a) Drain the cylinder and cylinder head.

(b) Disconnect the water outlet pipe from the cylinder head, and the water injection elbow.

(c) Remove the air cleaner, air inlet manifold and breather adaptor.

(d) Disconnect the exhaust pipe at the first joint.

(e) Disconnect the water inlet pipe from the cylinder head.

(f) Disconnect the rocker box oil pipe.

(g) Disconnect the fuel pipes and remove the fuel injector.

(h) Remove the rocker cover.

(j) Remove the rocker assembly and withdraw the push rods.

(k) Remove the cylinder head nuts and lift off the cylinder head.

D3—3 TO REMOVE VALVES

Hold the valve on the seat and depress the valve spring cap and remove the split collets. Valve and spring can now be removed.

D3—4 TO REMOVE CARBON

(a) Turn the crankshaft until the piston is at the top of its stroke.

(b) Scrape the carbon from the cylinder head and the top of the piston with a broad blunt tool. Emery cloth must NOT be used. Do not allow carbon dust to fall between the piston and the cylinder bore.

(c) Thoroughly clean out the exhaust and inlet ports and manifolds.

(d) DO NOT remove the air cell from the cylinder head. If a carbon deposit has formed in the air cell nozzle, it may be cleaned with a soft piece of wire.

(e) Make sure that the recesses at the end of the valve guide bores are free from carbon.

(f) Thoroughly clean the valves and examine the valve seats. If these show signs of pitting, they should be ground in.

(g) Make sure the valves are seating properly. Leaking valves cause loss of compression and difficult starting.

D3—5 TO REMOVE VALVE GUIDES

(a) EXTREME CARE AND CLEANLINESS is essential at all times when removing or replacing the valve guides.

(b) Thoroughly wash the cylinder head with petrol or paraffin to ensure that all carbon, oil and dirt has been removed.

(c) To remove the valve guides, place the cylinder head in boiling water for two minutes. Support the head on blocks at least ½ in. (12mm) thick, to prevent the valve guides bottoming. Press out the guides from the valve seat side with the aid of a hand press and punch.

(d) If a press is not available, a drift may be used, but SPECIAL CARE MUST BE TAKEN to avoid the drift slipping, scoring or otherwise damaging the bores.

(e) DO NOT USE EXCESSIVE FORCE if heavy resistance is encountered, but replace the cylinder head in boiling water for a further two minutes.

(f) When pressing out the guides ensure that the punch does not score or damage the bores in any way. Failure to observe this precaution may result in the new guides being loose in the cylinder head.

D3–6 TO REPLACE VALVE GUIDES

(a) Before fitting new guides, ensure the bores in the cylinder head and the body of the guides are clean.

(b) Place the cylinder head in boiling water for two minutes, enter the guides squarely in the bores from the rocker box side, and press home to the shoulder.

(c) If a press is not available, a drift may be used, but SPECIAL CARE MUST BE TAKEN to avoid the drift slipping, scoring or otherwise damaging the bores.

(d) The valve guides have a bonded coating and MUST NOT BE REAMED.

(e) Grind in the valves.

D3–7 TO GRIND IN VALVES

(a) Care must be taken that the valves are returned to their correct seating for this operation.

(b) Place a very small quantity of grinding paste evenly around the valve seat and insert the valve. Partially rotate the valve backwards and forwards on its seating, exerting a gentle but firm pressure.

(c) Periodically lift the valve from its seating and give it half a turn, thus ensuring that the grinding paste is evenly spread.

(d) It is unnecessary to continue grinding once the faces of the valve and its seating have a clean, even, matt-surfaced appearance. A polished surface must not be expected and is unnecessary.

(e) Wash out the ports thoroughly with petrol or paraffin making sure that all traces of grinding paste are removed from the valves and guides.

(f) Replace the valves and rotate them backwards and forwards a few times. If the valves have been correctly ground a thin polished line will appear all round the seat.

D3–8 TO REPLACE CYLINDER HEAD

(a) Generally reverse the instructions for removal and dismantling. The rocker bushes and push rod ends should be smeared with molybdenum-disulphide grease before assembly.

(b) It is IMPORTANT that the exhaust and inlet valves be returned to their correct positions.

(c) If the valves are distorted or very badly pitted, new ones must be fitted and ground in.

(d) If the valve guides show signs of wear or scoring, they should be replaced.

(e) Whenever the cylinder head is removed after the engine has been run, a new gasket MUST be fitted.

(f) As the engine is fitted with long through studs from crankcase to cylinder head it is MOST IMPORTANT that the cylinder head nuts are correctly tightened and in the right sequence.

(g) It is advisable to use a torque spanner for tightening the cylinder head nuts. It should be set to the figure shown under Technical Data. Proceed as follows:
  (i) Screw down each cylinder head nut until finger tight.
  (ii) Tighten each nut a quarter of a turn at a time, working diagonally across the cylinder head, until all the nuts are tight.
  (iii) After approximately 20 hours running check again for tightness.

(h) When reassembly is complete and before attempting to start the engine, bleed and prime the fuel system.

D3–9 TO ADJUST VALVE ROCKERS Fig. 2D

(a) To adjust the clearance, set the engine with valves closed (TDC of firing stroke), loosen the locknut (A) and turn the rocker adjusting screw (B) with a screwdriver. Measure the gap with a feeler gauge, and when the correct setting is obtained (see Technical Data) retighten the locknut. Recheck the gap.

(b) IMPORTANT. The cylinder head must be firmly bolted in position, with all nuts finally tightened, before the rocker clearances are adjusted.

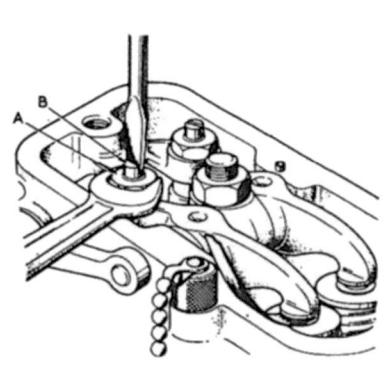
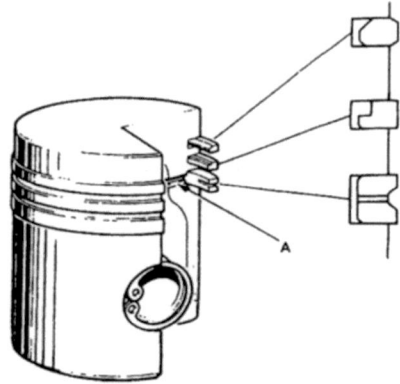

Fig. 2D Fig. 3D

D4–1 TO REMOVE CYLINDER AND PISTON
  (a) Remove the cylinder head.
  (b) Lift the cylinder off the crankcase and draw it off the piston.
  (c) To remove the piston, take out one gudgeon pin circlip and push out the gudgeon pin. If the gudgeon pin is a tight fit in the piston, wrap the piston in a cloth soaked in hot water. After a few minutes the gudgeon pin will be released and can be pushed out.

D4–2 CYLINDER MAINTENANCE
  (a) When the cylinder bore wear has reached the maximum it should be rebored and honed to the sizes shown under Technical Data, and an oversize piston and rings fitted.

D4–3 PISTON MAINTENANCE Fig. 3D
Excessive lubricating oil consumption, loss of compression and knocking are signs that a piston may need attention.
  (a) If the ring gaps are excessive (see Technical Data) the rings should be renewed. To measure the gaps remove the rings from the piston noting the order of assembly and which ring face is uppermost.
  (b) Remove all the carbon deposit from the rings and ring grooves. The small holes (A) in the scraper ring grooves should receive attention as their purpose is to return excess oil to the sump.
  (c) Insert the piston into the cylinder bore with the crown towards the bottom end of the bore to about ½in. (13mm) from the bottom edge. Insert the rings one at a time, pushing each ring hard up against the piston crown to ensure that it is level in the cylinder bore. Withdraw the piston sufficiently to allow the gap to be checked with a feeler gauge.
  (d) Assemble the rings on the piston in the correct order with the correct face uppermost. Rings should not be slack or stuck fast in the groove.
  (e) When the engine has been fully run-in, the bore will have a highly polished and very hard surface. If new rings are fitted without the cylinder being rebored or resleeved, the new rings will not bed in satisfactorily. Under these conditions the cylinder should be removed and the hard polished bore lightly roughened using a medium grade emery cloth. The roughening should be carried out radially, by hand, and should be sufficient only to produce a matt surface in the bore. After this treatment the cylinder must be thoroughly washed in petrol or paraffin to remove all traces of carborundum.

D4-4 TO REPLACE CYLINDER AND PISTON Fig. 3D
(a) Take care that the piston ring gaps are not in line, but well distributed around the piston circumference.
(b) Replace the shims between the cylinder and crankcase. The thickness of the shims controls the bumping clearance between the piston and cylinder head at TDC.
(c) Before completing reassembly check the bumping clearance (see Technical Data) as follows:
  (i) Insert a length of lead wire or soft solder through the injector port in the cylinder head. Pull through sufficient to allow approximately 1in. (25mm) to be positioned flat on the cylinder head between the inlet and exhaust valves. Wind any surplus wire around the injector studs.
  (ii) Replace the cylinder head, fitting a new gasket, and tighten the nuts in the correct sequence with a torque spanner.
  (iii) Turn the engine over TDC and then carefully remove the wire.
  (iv) Measure the thickness of the now flattened wire with a micrometer. If the clearance is outside the limit, adjust by changing one or more of the shims at the base of the cylinder, and recheck the bumping clearance.
(d) After completing reassembly, check the valve rocker clearance.

D5-1 TO EXAMINE CONNECTING ROD
(a) Remove cylinder head and cylinder.
(b) Check for undue play or shake in the large and small end bearings.

D5-2 TO REMOVE CONNECTING ROD
(a) Remove cylinder head and cylinder.
(b) Drain oil from engine sump.
(c) Remove the sump.
(d) Unscrew the large end bolts and withdraw the connecting rod and piston assembly, being careful to note in which position the bearing halves are fitted.

D5-3 CONNECTING ROD MAINTENANCE
(a) When fitting a small end bush take care that the oil hole coincides with that in the connecting rod and that the bush enters the connecting rod squarely. In the absence of a press, a block of wood and mallet may be used for driving it home.
(b) New small end bushes are supplied with a reaming allowance, and after fitting must be reamed to the size shown under Technical Data.
(c) Large end bearings are of the precision thin wall steel back type and consist of two half shells lined with bearing metal. They should be replaced in their original positions.
(d) New bearings are machined to give the required fit when in position and should not be scraped or bedded in, neither should shims of any description be fitted. If the faces of the connecting rod or its cap are filed the rod becomes useless regarding replacement bearing shells. When fitting, make sure that the connecting rod bore, the outside of the shells and their split faces are clean.
(e) Connecting rods and caps are stamped with an assembly serial number and care must be taken that numbers are correctly assembled and on the same side.
(f) Undersize bearings are obtainable.

D5-4 TO REPLACE CONNECTING ROD
(a) Generally reverse the instructions for removal, making sure that the connecting rod cap is away from the dipstick side of the engine.
(b) It is advisable to use a torque spanner for tightening the large end bolts. It should be set to the figure shown under Technical Data.
(c) Do not over-tighten the large end bolts or the bearing may distort. If a torque spanner is not available, the bolts may be tightened using a moderate force on a spanner gripped approximately 8in. (200mm) from the bolt.
(d) When replacing the cylinder and cylinder head, check the bumping clearance and valve rocker clearance.

D6—1 TO REMOVE FLYWHEEL
- (a) Remove the generator and bellhousing adaptor.
- (b) Secure the flywheel by inserting a hexagon wrench key or steel rod through the timing hole in the bellhousing, and locating it in the hole in the flywheel periphery. This rod must not be loose, but a good fit in the flywheel hole.
- (c) Bend back the tabwasher and remove the flywheel retaining nut.
- (d) Remove the securing rod.
- (e) A simple extractor will be required to remove the flywheel, as it is fitted on a tapered shaft and located by a key.
- (f) Remove the flywheel locating key.

D6—2 TO REPLACE FLYWHEEL
- (a) Generally reverse the instructions for removal.
- (b) Ensure that the flywheel locating key is replaced in the crankshaft before fitting the flywheel.
- (c) A new tabwasher must be fitted before tightening the flywheel retaining nut. It is advisable to use a torque spanner for tightening the flywheel nut, and should be set to the figure shown under Technical Data.
- (d) When the nut is tight, knock up the tabwasher.

D7—1 TO REMOVE CRANKSHAFT
- (a) Remove the cylinder head, cylinder, connecting rod and flywheel.
- (b) Remove the solenoid and starter motor, if fitted.
- (c) Remove the fuel and oil pipes, and place them in a clean container filled with clean fuel.
- (d) Remove the gear cover. This is dowelled to the crankcase.
- (e) Remove the crankshaft gearwheel retaining bolt. Withdraw the gear wheel with a simple extractor.
- (f) Remove the nuts retaining the flywheel end main bearing housing. Remove the housing taking care not to damage the oil seal.
- (g) Withdraw the crankshaft by pulling towards the flywheel end.

D7—2 CRANKSHAFT MAINTENANCE
- (a) Carefully examine the bearing journals and crankpin. They should be free from score marks and ovality should not exceed the maximum (see Technical Data).
- (b) If these defects are present the crankshaft should be reground to the diameter shown under Technical Data and undersize bearings fitted.
- (c) Carefully clean out the oil holes and make sure they have radiused edges.

D7—3 MAIN BEARING MAINTENANCE
- (a) Main bearings are of the precision thin wall steel backed sleeve type lined with bearing metal.
- (b) When removing a gear end bearing from the crankcase or a flywheel end bearing from the bearing housing, heat the crankcase or bearing housing to a temperature of 93/120°C (200/250°F) before pressing out the bearing.
- (c) When fitting a bearing, the crankcase or bearing housing should again be heated as above and the outer surface of the bearing should be smeared with molybdenum-disulphide grease or tallow before pressing in. It is an advantage if the bearing can be placed in a domestic type refrigerator for a time before fitting.
- (d) Do not remove the bearings unnecessarily or their tightness in the crankcase or bearing housing may be affected. It is not advisable to remove the bearings more than five times.
- (e) When fitting a bearing take care that it enters squarely.
- (f) New bearings are machined to give the required fit when in position and should not be scraped or bedded in, neither should shims of any description be fitted.
- (g) Undersize bearings are obtainable.

D7—4 TO REPLACE CRANKSHAFT AND TIME ENGINE Figs. 4D and 5D.
- (a) Generally reverse the instructions for removal.
- (b) Fit new bearings if the old ones have excessive clearance or show signs of the metal having run.
- (c) If the main bearing housing has been removed make sure it is correctly fitted with the oil drain hole at the bottom.

(d) When fitting new thrust washers, be sure that the grooved sides are away from the bearing housing and that the tongues (A) are located in their respective recesses. Fit new pins (B).
(e) Before completing the assembly, check the end float (Y) and if excessive fit new thrust washers (see Technical Data).
(f) When assembling the gearwheels make sure that the teeth marked with dots are in their relative positions.
(g) Tighten the crankshaft gearwheel retaining screw and extension shaft screws, if fitted, using a torque spanner set to the figure shown under Technical Data.
(h) AC1W. Proceed as follows:
   (i) Loosely fit the crankcase-to-rocker-box oil pipe at the crankcase end. Feed the crankcase-to-main-bearing-housing oil pipe through the flywheel guard and loosely attach to the crankcase-to-rocker-box oil pipe banjo.
   (ii) Fit the pipe to the main bearing housing union and tighten the nut.
   (iii) Remove the crankcase-to-rocker-box oil pipe.
(j) Replace the flywheel.
(k) If a starting arrangement is fitted to the gear cover, maintenance should be carried out before replacing.
(l) If a water pump is fitted, ensure that the impeller is correctly fitted to the shaft.
(m) Before completing reassembly, check the bumping clearance.

D7–5 CRANKCASE BREATHER MAINTENANCE

Under normal circumstances the breather assembly will not require maintenance. However, if removal is necessary proceed as follows:
(a) Turn off the fuel supply.
(b) Remove the breather pipe, cover and valve.
(c) Remove the breather housing and seal from the crankcase. A special tool for this purpose is available
(d) Thoroughly clean all parts in paraffin or clean fuel.
(e) Examine the seal and valve for damage and replace if necessary.
(f) When fitting the cover, ensure that the pipe connection is parallel to the crankshaft and facing the flywheel end.

D8–1 TO REMOVE CAMSHAFT Fig. 6D.

(a) Drain the engine sump.
(b) Remove the starter motor.
(c) Remove fuel injection pump. Cover holes in injector against admission of dirt, etc.
(d) Remove the water pump, and gear cover.
(e) Remove the rocker cover, rocker support and rocker assembly and withdrawn the push rods.
(f) Turn the engine onto its side to prevent the tappets from falling into the sump.
(g) Remove the extension shaft from the camshaft gearwheel.
(h) Remove the screw (A) retaining the camshaft thrust plate. These are accessible through holes in the gearwheel. Withdraw the camshaft and gearwheel assembly from the gear end of the engine.
(j) The gearwheel is a tight fit on the camshaft. To fit a new thrust plate, remove the gearwheel retaining bolt and press the shaft from the gearwheel. The gearwheel is keyed to the shaft.

D8–2 CAMSHAFT MAINTENANCE

(a) Carefully examine the faces of the cams. If these are worn or chipped it will be necessary to fit a new camshaft.

D8–3 TO REPLACE CAMSHAFT AND TIME ENGINE Figs. 5D and 7D.

(a) Generally reverse instructions for removal.
(b) Check the camshaft end float (Y) and if excessive fit a new thrust plate (see Technical Data).
(c) When assembling the gearwheels make sure that the teeth marked with dots are in their relative positions.
(d) Tighten the camshaft gearwheel retaining screw and extension shaft screws, if fitted, using a torque spanner set to the figure shown under Technical Data.
(e) Retime the fuel injection pump and adjust the valve clearances.

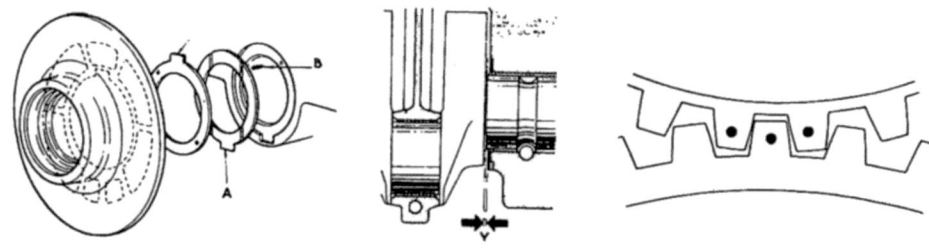

Fig. 4D   Fig. 5D

D9–1 TO REMOVE GOVERNOR Fig. 8D.
   (a)   Remove the water pump, and gear cover.
   (b)   Remove the screws (A) securing the governor assembly to the crankcase and withdraw it.

D9–2 TO REMOVE GOVERNOR LINKAGE Fig. 8D.
   (a)   Remove the governor.
   (b)   Remove the gearwheel from the camshaft.
   (c)   Move the stop/run lever (B) to the 'RUN' position, i.e. horizontal.
   (d)   Remove the screws (C) securing the governor stop cover (D), or speed control bracket if fitted and remove it.
   (e)   Loosen the governor bracket screw (E) and remove the bracket (F), speeder spring and speeder spring plunger.
   (f)   Remove the breather assembly (G) and withdraw the shaft (H) and fuel pump operating lever (J).
   (g)   If oil is leaking from the overload stop spindle or the return spring is damaged remove the pin (K) securing the overload stop lever (L) and remove the lever. The spindle and return spring (P) can now be withdrawn from the inside of the crankcase.

NOTE: The overload stop assembly is not fitted to fixed speed engines.

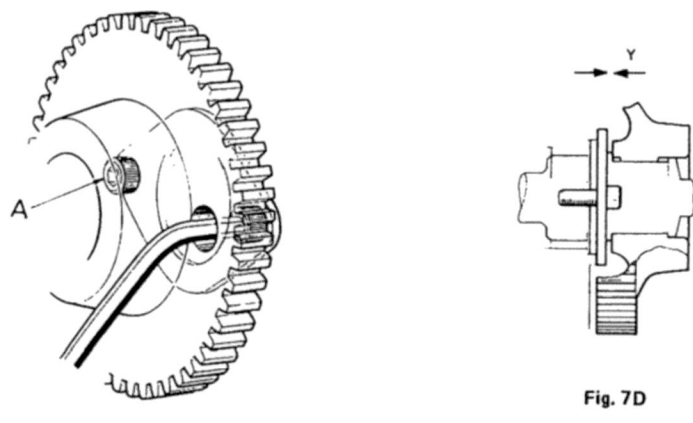

Fig. 6D   Fig. 7D

D9–3 GOVERNOR AND LINKAGE MAINTENANCE Fig. 8D.
   (a)   Thoroughly clean all parts in paraffin or clean fuel, paying particular attention to all bearings and governor balls.
   (b)   Examine the faces of the governor sliding and rotating housings for signs of wear. If worn, the governor assembly must be replaced.
   (c)   If oil leaks at the stop/run lever spindle (R), carefully remove the spindle and renew the oil seal. When refitting the spindle ensure that it is free from burrs.

D9-4 TO REPLACE GOVERNOR AND LINKAGE Fig. 8D.

(a) Generally reverse the instructions for removal.
(b) Ensure that the fuel pump lever fork end is correctly located on the fuel pump rack ball (S).
(c) Applicable to variable speed engines only.

Before replacing the overload stop assembly, adjust the governor linkage to the correct position as follows:—

    (i) With the governor bracket screw (E) loose, make sure that the governor bracket fork ends are hard against the governor thrust bearing when the faces of the governor sliding and rotating housings are together.
    (ii) Push the fuel pump operating lever as far as possible to the fuel pump fully open position.
    (iii) Tighten the governor bracket locking screw.
    (iv) Check the setting (X) between the operating shaft bush and the operating lever with a feeler gauge. This should be 0.010in. (0.25mm).

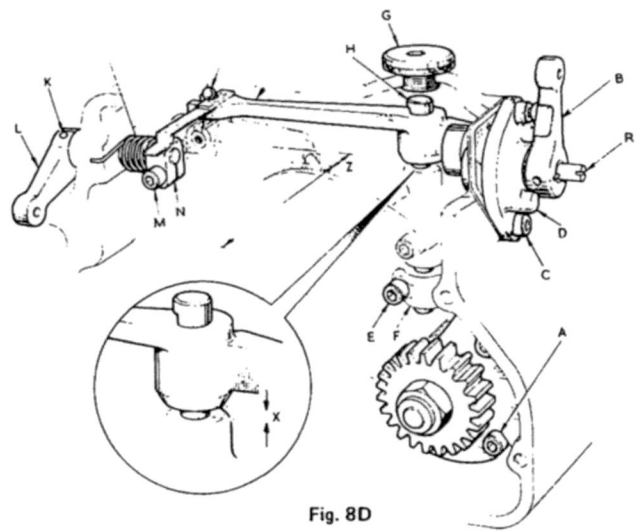

Fig. 8D

D10-1 LUBRICATING OIL SYSTEM Fig. 9D.

(a) The lubricating oil system is as follows:—
    (i) A rotary oil pump (A) is mounted in the crankcase at the gear end. The pump is driven by a gear from the camshaft.
    (ii) Oil is drawn through a strainer (B) and fed to the filter (C).
    (iii) Oil flows from the filter via a hole in the crankcase to the gear end main bearing. It is then transferred via holes in the crankshaft to the large end bearing and the flywheel end main bearing.
    (iv) The valve rockers are supplied by an external pipe.
    (v) A pressure relief valve is incorporated to control the oil pressure.
(b) The cylinder, small end bearing and camshaft are splash lubricated.
(c) The crankcase can be drained by removing the plug at the bottom of the sump.
(d) Oil must always be CLEAN and containers, funnels, etc., must be kept in a spotless conditi Use only approved oil. Cheap, unsuitable or dirty oil will cause trouble.

D10-2 TO CLEAN OIL FILTER

(a) Unscrew the bolt at the centre of the filter cover and withdraw the cover and element.
(b) Thoroughly clean out the cover and renew the joint ring.
(c) If the element shows a large deposit of dirt, it should be renewed. Do not attempt to clean the element.
(d) When replacing the element, it is advisable to use a torque spanner for tightening the centre bolt. It should be set to the figure shown under Technical Data.

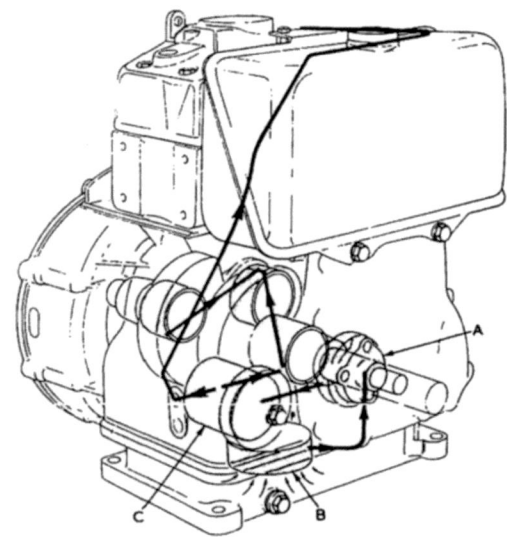

Fig. 9D

D10—3 OIL PUMP STRAINER
- (a) To remove
  - (i) Drain oil from the sump.
  - (ii) Remove sump.
  - (iii) Remove the centre bolt and spring plate and remove the strainer.
- (b) To clean, wash the strainer in clean paraffin or fuel.
- (c) To replace, generally reverse the instructions for removal, making sure that the strainer is correctly seated in the sump.

D10—4 TO REMOVE OIL PUMP
- (a) Drain the engine sump.
- (b) Remove the water pump, raised hand starting assembly (if fitted) and gear cover.
- (c) Loosen the oil pump gearwheel retaining nut.
- (d) Remove the camshaft and gearwheel assembly.
- (e) Remove the nut retaining the oil pump gearwheel and remove the gearwheel. The gearwheel is keyed to the shaft.
- (f) Remove the screws securing the pump and withdraw the pump.
- (g) The backplate is dowelled to the body.

D10—5 OIL PUMP MAINTENANCE
- (a) Thoroughly clean all parts.
- (b) Carefully examine the rotor and stator. If they are scored or show signs of wear fit new parts.

D10—6 TO REPLACE OIL PUMP
- (a) Generally reverse the instructions for removal.
- (b) Pour a small quantity of engine oil into the pump through the port before assembling the pump to the engine.
- (c) It is advisable to use a torque spanner for tightening the oil pump screws. It should be set to the figure shown under Technical Data.

D11–1 FUEL SYSTEM

(a) Fuel from the tank flows through a filter to the injection pump which supplies it under high pressure to the injector.

(b) A small amount of fuel is always leaking back along the injector nozzle needle and this is returned to the fuel system by a pipe.

(c) The quantity of fuel injected during each cycle is very small and the fuel injection equipment is manufactured to very fine limits. IT REQUIRES EXTREME CARE AND ABSOLUTE CLEANLINESS IN HANDLING.

(d) Should any part of the fuel system, including pipes, be removed from the engine, it should be placed in a clean container which is filled with clean fuel. NO FILING, GRINDING, SCRAPING OR SAWING SHOULD BE CARRIED OUT WITHIN A FEW YARDS OF DISMANTLED FUEL INJECTION EQUIPMENT.

(e) Replace the equipment wet. No rag, cloth or waste should touch it.

(f) Unless the user has been trained in the care and repair of fuel injection equipment, he should not dismantle it in any way other than as described in subsequent paragraphs.

(g) Fuel pumps and injectors should be returned to an authorised agent for repair or replacement. Users are advised to keep a nozzle in their spares kit so that a faulty one can be renewed immediately.

D11–2 TO CLEAN FUEL FILTER (SEPARATELY MOUNTED FUEL TANK)

(a) Turn off the fuel supply.

(b) Unscrew the clamp bolt at the centre of the filter bowl and withdraw the bowl complete with element.

(c) Thoroughly clean out the bowl and examine the joint ring.

(d) If the element shows a large deposit of dirt, fit a new element. Do not attempt to clean the element.

(e) It is advisable to fit a new joint ring when the element is changed.

(f) Reassemble the filter and turn on the fuel.

(g) Bleed and prime the fuel system.

D11–3 TO REMOVE FUEL INJECTION PUMP

(a) Turn off the fuel supply.

(b) Remove the solenoid and starter, if fitted.

(c) Remove the tank-to-pump and pump-to-injector fuel pipes.

(d) Remove the pump, noting the number and total thickness of shims between the fuel pump and crankcase.

D11–4 TO DISMANTLE FUEL INJECTION PUMP Fig. 10D.

Fixed speed engines

(a) Thoroughly clean the exterior of the pump.

(b) Unscrew the union body (A) and lift out the delivery valve spring (B) and the delivery valve (C).

(c) Withdraw the delivery valve seat (D), the joint (E) and the ring (F).

(d) Rotate the circlip (G) in its groove until the dowel (H) is between the ends of the circlip.

(e) Press down the tappet and roller assembly against the spring pressure and shake out the dowel (H).

(f) Remove the tappet (J) together with the roller and roller pin. Note the number and thickness of the calibrating shims (K) between the tappet and the lower spring plate (L).

(g) Remove the lower spring plate (L), the plunger (M) and the plunger spring (N). Note the assembly mark on the plunger arm farthest from the rack (P).

(h) Remove the upper spring plate (R) and the pinion (S). Note the assembly marks on one tooth of the pinion (S) and on the rack (P). Note also the relative position of the 'STOP' mark and arrow on the rack before sliding out the rack from the pump body.

(j) Remove the element locating screw (T) and push out the element (U) through the top of the pump.

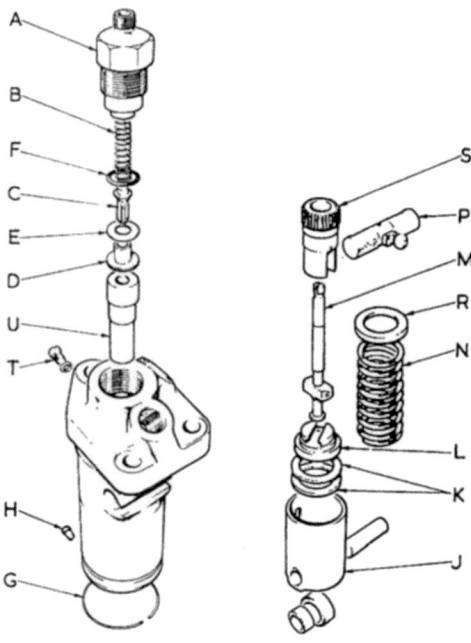

Fig. 10D

D11–5 FUEL INJECTION PUMP MAINTENANCE

(a) Each plunger of a pump assembly is mated to one element and must never be used i another.

(b) Make sure the delivery valve joint and ring are in good condition and that the valve is seating correctly. Leaking valves cause loss of fuel injection pressure and difficult starting.

(c) Make sure the rack is free throughout its travel.

D11–6 TO REPLACE FUEL INJECTION PUMP Fig. 10D.

(a) Generally reverse the instructions for removal and dismantling.

(b) Thoroughly clean all parts in clean fuel and assemble wet.

(c) The ring (F) should be fitted over the lower shoulder of the union body (A) before the union body is screwed into the pump body. Failure to observe this precaution may result in the ring being crushed between the union body and the joint (E). A torque spanner is advisable for tightening the union body. It should be set to the figure shown under Technical Data.

(d) When assembling the rack (P) and pinion (S) make sure that the marked tooth of the pinion is opposite the mark on the rack and that the rack is assembled in the pump body so that the 'STOP' mark and arrow will be towards the gear end of the engine when the pump is fitted.

(e) Make sure that the element (U) can be moved up and down slightly when the locating screw (T) is tightened.

(f) Replace the plunger (M) with the marked locating arm engaged with the marked slot in the pinion (S), i.e., the marked locating arm is towards the locating screw (T).

(g) With the element, plunger and pinion correctly assembled, the scroll at the top of the plunger will be adjacent to the fuel port in the side of the element when the rack is in the centre of its travel.

(h) Replace the tappet (J) making sure that the correct number and thickness of shims is used.

(j) Press down the tappet and roller assembly and fit the dowel (H) to engage with the slot in the tappet. Rotate the dowel to line up its slot with the ends of the circlip (G) and then turn the circlip in its groove until the ends of the circlip are away from the dowel.

- (k) Make sure that the fuel pump cam is away from the fuel pump housing – turn the engine until the exhaust or inlet valve is open.
- (l) Make sure that the fuel pump rack ball engages with the governor fork and that the correct number and thickness of shims is fitted between the pump and crankcase.
- (m) IMPORTANT. New fuel injection pumps require special fitting instructions and these are given in the following paragraph.

D11–7 TO FIT NEW FUEL INJECTION PUMP Fig. 8D.

Fixed speed engines

- (a) Make sure that the fuel pump cam is at the bottom of its stroke. Turn the engine until the exhaust or inlet valve is open.
- (b) Turn the STOP/RUN lever (B) until the governor lever fork end is at the centre of the fuel pump housing.
- (c) Fit the fuel pump. Make sure that the fuel pump rack ball (S) has engaged with the governor lever fork.
- (d) Time the fuel injection pump.

D11–8 TO TIME FUEL INJECTION PUMP Fig. 10 and 11D.

- (a) Before timing the pump be sure the fuel line is bled up to the fuel pump.
- (b) On all AC1W engines, move the stop/run lever to the 'RUN' position, i.e. horizontal.
- (c) Remove the pump-to-injector pipe and unscrew the union body from the pump.
- (d) Unscrew the delivery union body (A) and remove, making sure that the sealing ring (F) is withdrawn also. Lift out the delivery valve (C) and spring (B), placing them in clean fuel. Do not disturb the delivery valve seat (D) or joint washer (E).
- (e) Position the sealing ring on the delivery union body and replace in the pump body leaving out the delivery valve and spring. Replace the pump-to-injector pipe, connecting the pump end only.
- (f) With the decompressor lever disengaged, turn the flywheel until it is a quarter of a turn before TDC on the compression stroke. A small stream of fuel should now flow from the pump-to-injector pipe.
- (g) Engage the decompressor lever and turn the flywheel slowly by hand in a clockwise direction until the flow from the pipe stops. Find by repeated trial the EXACT flywheel position at which this happens. This position is known as the spill point.
- (h) Read off the angle through the timing hole at the mark on the bellhousing. Check this with the figure shown under Technical Data. If the angle is too large, add shims between the pump and crankcase until the correct timing is obtained. If too small, remove shims.
- (j) When the correct timing is obtained, reassemble the fuel injection equipment including the fuel delivery valve and spring. Ensure that the union body sealing ring is not damaged and is located on the union body shoulder before replacing in the pump.
- (k) Tighten the delivery union body using a torque spanner set to the figure shown under Technical Data.

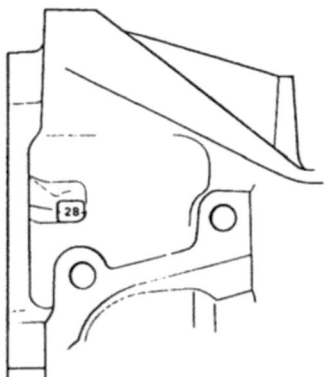

Fig. 11D

D11-9 TO REMOVE AND TEST FUEL INJECTOR

(a) Disconnect the fuel feed and leak-off pipes from the injector.
(b) Remove the injector flange nuts and carefully lever out the injector and the nozzle shield washer. Examine the joint washer and renew if necessary.
(c) Reconnect the injector to the pump-to-injector pipe in such a way that the nozzle poi away from the engine.
(d) With the stop/run lever in the 'RUN' position turn the engine over slowly. The fuel should squirt out suddenly in a fine mist spray which should stop as suddenly. If the nozzle fails to spray or gives a solid squirt of fuel, or dribbles after the spray has stopped, fit a new nozzle.
(e) When testing, BE CAREFUL to see that the spray is not directed at any exposed part of the body. The force behind the spray will cause it to penetrate the skin.

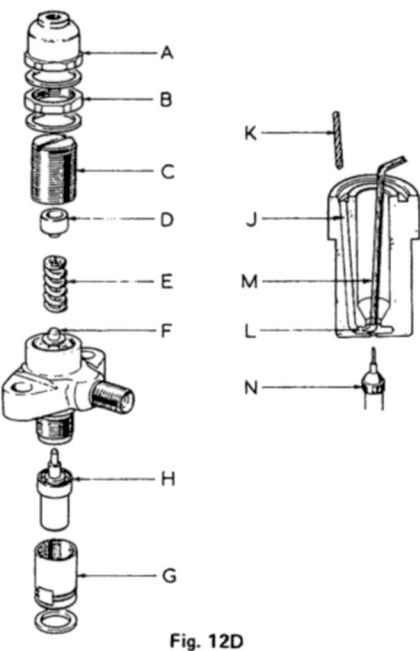

Fig. 12D

D11-10 FUEL INJECTOR MAINTENANCE Fig. 12D.

(a) Thoroughly clean the exterior of the injector.
(b) Remove the nozzle holder cap nut (A) and the locknut (B).
(c) Remove the spring adjusting screw (C) and remove the spring pad (D), the spring (E) and the spring pressure rod (F).
(d) Remove the nozzle nut (G) and the nozzle assembly (H). Each needle of a nozzle assembly is mated to one nozzle body and must never be used in another.
(e) To ensure a thorough cleaning of all parts they should be left in a bath of clean fuel. After this treatment, any remaining carbon can be scraped off with a soft brass wire brush or a piece of clean wood or brass.
(f) The nozzle holder and nozzle joint faces must be clean with mirror-like appearance. The nozzle and nozzle nut clamping shoulders must be clean.
(g) The nozzle body fuel holes (J) should be cleaned by pushing a wire or twist drill (K) down to the fuel chamber (L) being careful not to scratch the joint face.
(h) Insert a nozzle scraper (M) down into the fuel chamber, press sideways and rotate to remove carbon, etc.
(j) Soft carbon can be removed from the spray hole with a spray hole cleaner (N).
(k) Wash the nozzle body and needle in clean fuel and assemble wet.

(l) To fit a nozzle assembly to the nozzle holder body, hold it hard against the pressure face and tighten the nozzle nut.

(m) To complete the assembly of the injector, grease the spring assembly and replace it, together with the adjuster, locknut and cap nut.

(n) Reset the fuel injector release pressure to the figure shown under Technical Data. To adjust the release pressure, loosen the locknut (B) and screw in the adjusting screw (C) to increase the pressure, or out to decrease it. Tighten the locknut.

(p) Injectors not required for immediate use should have pipe connections sealed against the admission of dirt, etc.

D11-11 TO REPLACE FUEL INJECTOR Fig. 13D.

(a) It is MOST IMPORTANT that the pump-to-injector pipe is correctly fitted or the pipe and injector may be damaged.
A new nozzle shield washer (A) MUST be fitted before the injector (B) is replaced. This washer must be fitted so that the dimple side is away from the injector nozzle.

(b) Loosely fit the injector flange nuts.

(c) Fit the pipe and tighten the union nuts finger tight, then give them a third of a turn with a spanner.

(d) Tighten the injector flange nuts evenly. It is advisable to use a torque spanner for tightening the nuts. It should be set to the figure shown under Technical Data.

(e) Reconnect the leak-off pipe.

(f) Bleed the fuel system.

D12-1 TO ADJUST SPEED CONTROL Fig. 14D.

Loosen the locknut (C) on the dipstick side of the engine and screw in the adjuster (B) to increase the speed or out to decrease it. Tighten the locknut.

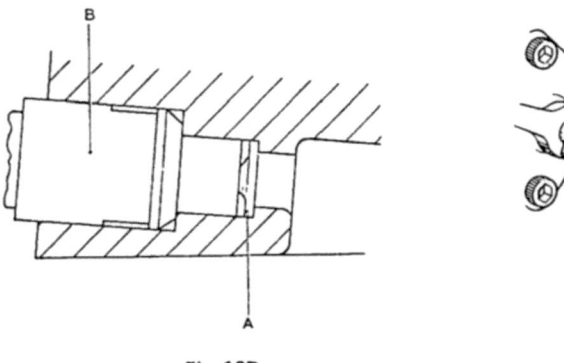

Fig. 13D   Fig. 14D

D13-1 AIR CLEANER MAINTENANCE

Paper element type

(a) Unscrew the nut on the cover and remove the cover.

(b) Remove the element. The element may be cleaned by blowing compressed air from the inside to the outside. Do not attempt to clean the element by any other means.

(c) A strong light directed into the inside of an element and viewed from the outside will reveal any damage to the paper corrugations. If the element is damaged or shows a large deposit of dirt, fit a new element.

(d) Thoroughly wash out the cover in petrol or paraffin and allow to drain. Make sure the gauze is clean.

(e) Dip the cover in a bath of clean engine oil and allow to drain.

(f) Replace the element and cover making sure that the element sealing rings and inlet manifold seal are in good condition.

D14–1 STARTER MOTOR – WHERE FITTED

(a) **Mounting**
Make sure the motor is securely mounted on the engine.

(b) **Lubrication**
Bearings are lubricated on assembly and require no attention between overhaul periods.

(c) **Terminals**
Main terminals and all circuit connections must be clean and tight. Terminal shrouds should be in position.

(d) **Brush gear**
Remove the cover and inspect the brushes and commutator. Brushes should be free in their slides. Springs should seat squarely on the brushes. See that the insulation is in good condition. The brushes and commutator should be free from dust and grease and contact surfaces clean, smooth and uniform in colour.

(e) **Solenoid**
The solenoid should move freely and contact faces be clean and unburnt. Do not attempt to clean the solenoid without disconnecting the battery.

D15–1 FAULT LOCATING CHART

Engine will not start

Reason	Causes	Suggested Remedy
Low temperature	Failure to prime (see Cold Starting)	Prime with lubricating oil
Fuel supply failure Check by turning engine and listen for the characteristic squeak in the injector	No fuel in tank) Air in pipe line) Broken fuel pipe or leaking connection Fuel filter choked Faulty injector nozzle Fuel pump plunger sticking Fuel pump tappet sticking	Fill tank and bleed fuel system, if applicable Repair or renew the pipe or tighten the connection Fit new fuel filter element Fit new nozzle Fit new pump Free and clean tappet
Poor compressi	Valves sticking Cylinder head loose Cylinder head gasket blown Piston rings stuck in groove Worn cylinder and piston Valves not seating properly	Free the valves Tighten all nuts Fit new gasket Check rings and clean the piston Overhaul the engine (Check valve springs (Grind in if necessary (Check the valve clearance
Incorrect lubricating oil	Too high a viscosity oil causing excessive engine drag	Drain the sump and fill with correct oil.

Engine starts but fires intermittently or soon stops

Reason	Causes	Suggested Remedy
Faulty fuel supply	Water in the fuel Faulty injector nozzle Fuel filter choked Air in fuel pipes	Drain fuel system and fill with clean fuel Fit new nozzle Fit new filter element Bleed the system, if applicable
Faulty compression	Broken valve spring Sticking valve Pitted valve	Fit new spring Free the valve Grind or renew
Dirty exhaust	Blocked exhaust pipe or similar	Clean out

Engine lacks power and/or shows dirty exhaust

Faulty fuel supply	Faulty fuel pump	Fit new pump
	Faulty Injector nozzle	Fit new nozzle
	Unsuitable fuel	Drain the fuel system and fill with correct fuel
Out of adjustment	Valve clearances incorrect	Adjust
	Fuel timing incorrect	Adjust
Dirty engine	Blocked exhaust pipe or similar	Clean out
	Dirty air cleaner	Clean out
	Faulty piston ring	Fit new ring
	Excessive carbon on piston and cylinder head	Decarbonise
	Worn cylinder or piston	Overhaul the engine

Faulty running

Knocking	Carbon on piston crown	Decarbonise
	Injector needle sticking	Fit new nozzle
	Fuel timing too far advanced	Adjust timing
	Broken piston ring	Fit new ring
	Slack piston	Fit new piston rings
	Worn large end bearing	Renew and check lubri
	Loose flywheel	Refit
	Worn main bearing	Renew and check lubricati
Overheating	Cooling system failure:	Check for leaks or blockages
	Suction pipe blocked	Remove and clean
	Air leak in suction pipe	Check and tighten fittings
	Broken water pump rotor	Replace rotor and check pump
	Faulty water pump seal	Replace seal and check pump
	Overloaded	Reduce the load
	Excessive valve clearance	Adjust
	Lubricating oil failure	Check the engine and lubricating oil system for damage. If in order, top up sump and check running.
Speed surges	Overheating	See above
	Air in fuel pipes	Bleed the system, if applicable
	Governor sticking	Check the governor for correct operation.
Sudden stop	Empty fuel tank	Fill tank and bleed system, if applicable.
	Choked injector	Fit new nozzle
	Fuel pipe broken	Repair or renew
	Seized piston	Fit new cylinder and piston
Heavy vibration	Faulty installation	Check holding down bolts and flexible mountings and couplings if fitted.

SECTION E

SPARE PARTS LISTS

E1	CRANKCASE
E2	CYLINDER AND CYLINDER HEAD
E3	CAMSHAFT AND GOVERNOR
E4	FLYWHEEL CRANKCASE AND PISTON
E5	FUEL AND OIL PIPES
E6	FUEL FILTER
E7	FUEL PUMP
E8	AIR CLEANER
E9	OIL PUMP AND FILTER
E10	WATER PUMP
E11	RAISED HAND STARTING
E12	SERVICING KITS
E13	SPEEDER SPRING DETAILS
E14	COMMON DETAIL PARTS
E15	GENERAL ASSEMBLY

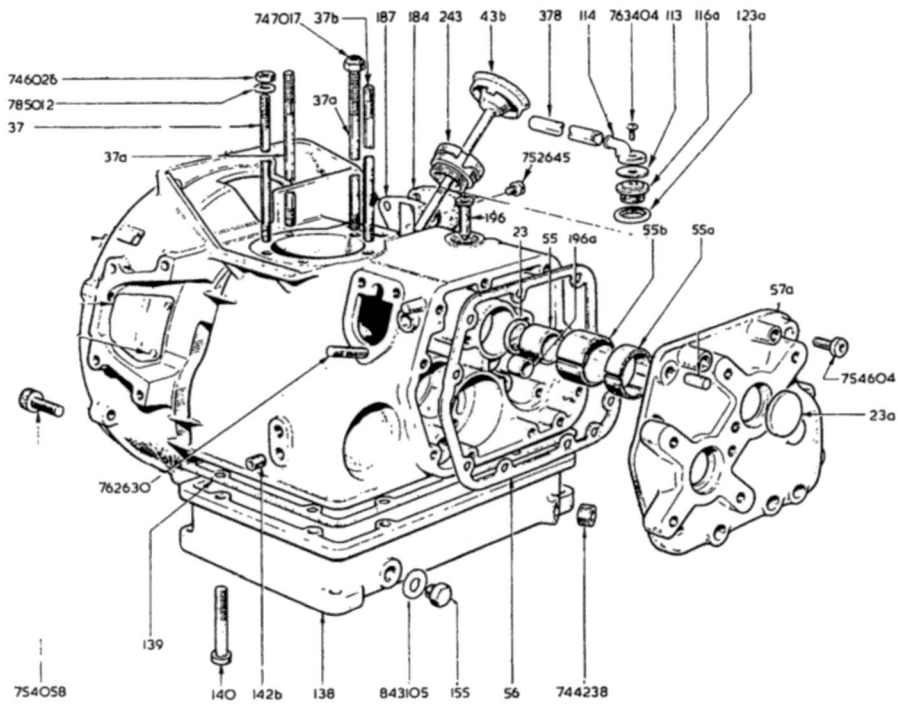

E1 CRANKCASE

Ref. No.	Description	AC1W
AAA23	Plug – Camshaft Bore (Flywheel end)	1
AAA23a	Plug – Gear Cover	1
ACA36c	Crankcase, complete with Camshaft Bushes, Fuel Pump Lever Operating Shaft Bush, Governor Shaft Bush and Gear End Main Bearing	1
ACA37a	Stud – Cylinder Head (Long)	2
ACA37	Stud – Cylinder Head (Short)	2
ACA43b	Dipstick, complete with Oil Filler Cap	1
AAA55	Bearing – Camshaft (Flywheel end)	1
AAA55a	Bearing – Camshaft (Gear end)	1
AAA55b	Bearing – Camshaft (Intermediate)	1
AAA56	Joint – Gear Cover (Supplied only in Sets of Joints)	1
AAA57	Cover – Gear	1
ABA57e	Cover – Gear (Flange Mounting)	1
AAA62	Dowel – Gear Cover	2
ACA113	Valve – Breather	1
ACA114	Cover – Breather	1
ACA116a	Housing – Breather	1
ACA123a	Oil Seal – Breather	1
ACA138	Sump	1
AAA139	Joint – Sump (Supplied only in Sets of Joints)	1
ACA140	Screw – Sump	8
AAA142b	Plug – Crankcase Oilway	1
AAA196	Bush – Fuel Pump Lever Operating Shaft	1
AAA196a	Bush – Governor Shaft	1
AAA243	Collar – Oil Filler	1
ACA378	Pipe – Breather	1

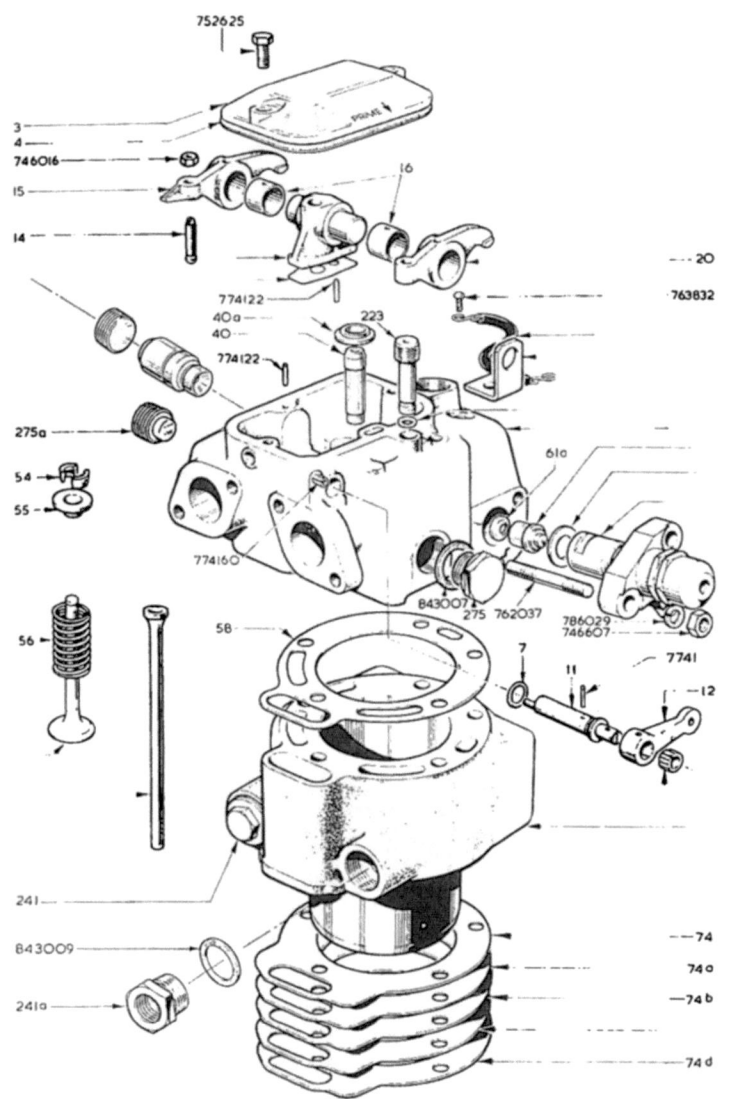

E2

E2 CYLINDER AND CYLINDER HEAD

Ref. No.	Descripti	AC1W
AAB3	Cover — Rocker Box	1
AAB4	Joint — Rocker Box Cover (Supplied only in Sets of Joints)	1
AAB7	Oil Seal — Decompressor Shaft	1
AAB11	Shaft — Decompressor	1
AAB12	Lever — Decompressor	1
AAB14	Screw — Valve Rocker Adjusting	2
ABB15	Rocker — Exhaust Valve	1
AAB16	Bush — Valve Rocker	2
ABB20	Rocker — Inlet Valve	1
ABB32	Support — Rocker	1
AAB33	Joint — Rocker Support	1
ACB39C	Cylinder Head, complete with Valve Guides, Valve Inserts, Valves, Valve Springs, Air Cell and Plug	1
ABB40	Guide — Valve	2
ABB40a	Spring Plate — Valve Guide	2
ABB53	Valve	2
ABB54	Collet — Valve	2 prs.
ABB55	Cup — Valve	2
ABB56	Spring — Valve	2
ACB58	Gasket — Cylinder Head (Supplied only in Sets of Joints)	1
ACB59	Holder — Fuel Injector Nozzle	1
AAB60	Nozzle — Fuel Injector	1
ACB61a	Washer — Nozzle Shield (Supplied only with Fuel Injector Nozzle or in Sets of Joints)	1
ACB69b	Cylinder	1
WAB74	Shim — Cylinder (0.003")	As required
WAB74a	Shim — Cylinder (0.005")	As required
WAB74b	Shim — Cylinder (0.010")	As required
WAB74c	Shim — Cylinder (0.015")	As required
WAB74d	Shim — Cylinder (0.020")	As required
AAB197	Bracket — Lifting	1
ACB203	Push Rod — Valve	2
AAB223	Plunger — Priming	1
AAB224	Oil Seal — Priming Plunger	1
WAB241	Plug — Cylinder	1
WAB241	Plug — Cylinder (Water Pump)	1
WAB241a	Bush — Reducing	1
AAB251	Chain — Priming Plunger	1
AAB256	Bush — Decompressor Shaft	1
WAB275	Plug — Cylinder Head	1
WAB275a	Plug — Corrosion Inhibitor	1

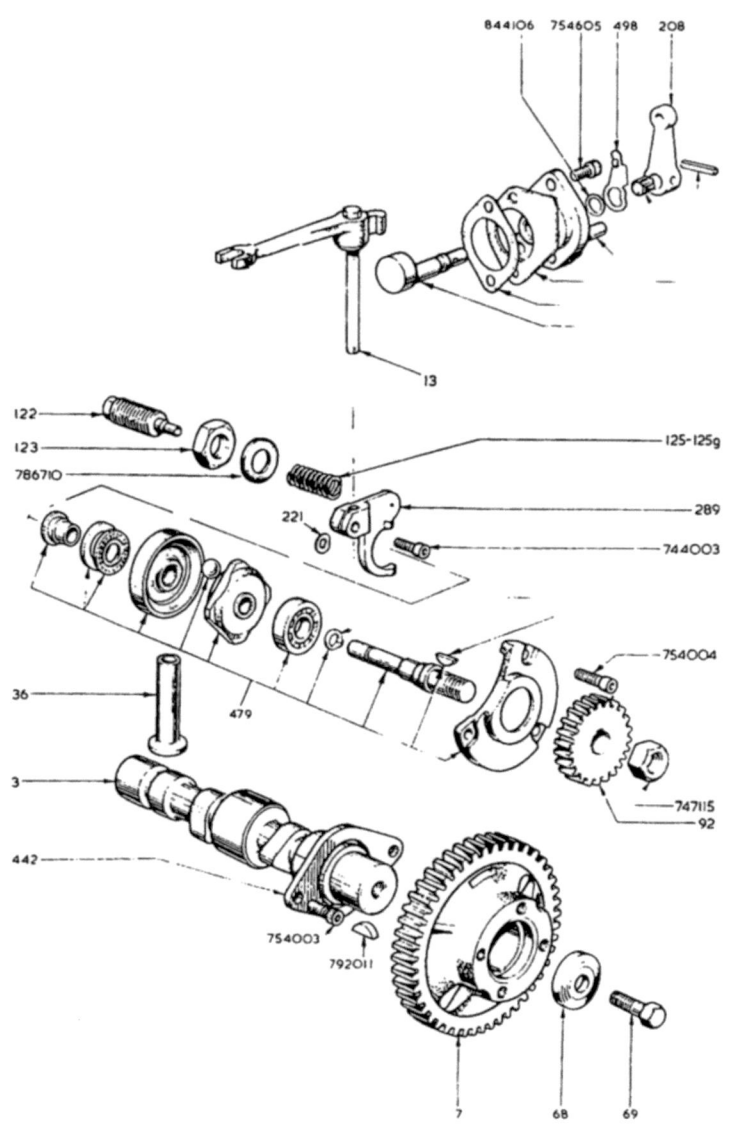

E3

E3 CAMSHAFT, GOVERNOR AND LINKAGE, STOP/RUN AND FIXED SPEED CONTROLS

Ref. No.	Description	AC1W
ACD3	Camshaft ...	1
ACD7	Gearwheel — Camshaft	1
AAD13	Shaft — Lever Operating ...	1
AAD14	Lever — Fuel Pump Operating	1
AAD36	Tappet — Valve	2
AAD68	Plate — Gearwheel Retaining	1
AAD69	Screw — Gearwheel Retaining	1
AAD92	Gearwheel — Governor	1
AAD122	Adjuster — Speeder Spring	1
AAD123	Locknut — Speeder Spring Adjuster	1
AAD125g	Spring — Speeder (for details see separate list)	1
AAD201	Bush — Stop/Run Lever	1
AAD202	Spindle — Stop/Run Lever	1
AAD208	Lever — Stop/Run	1
AAD221	Spacer — Governor Bracket ...	1
AAD253	Cover — Stop/Run Lever Assembly	1
AAD256	Joint — Cover (Supplied only in Sets of Joints)	1
AAD289	Bracket — Governor	1
AAD478	Plate — Stop/Run	1
AAD479	Governor Assembly	1
AAD498	Spring — Stop/Run Lever	1

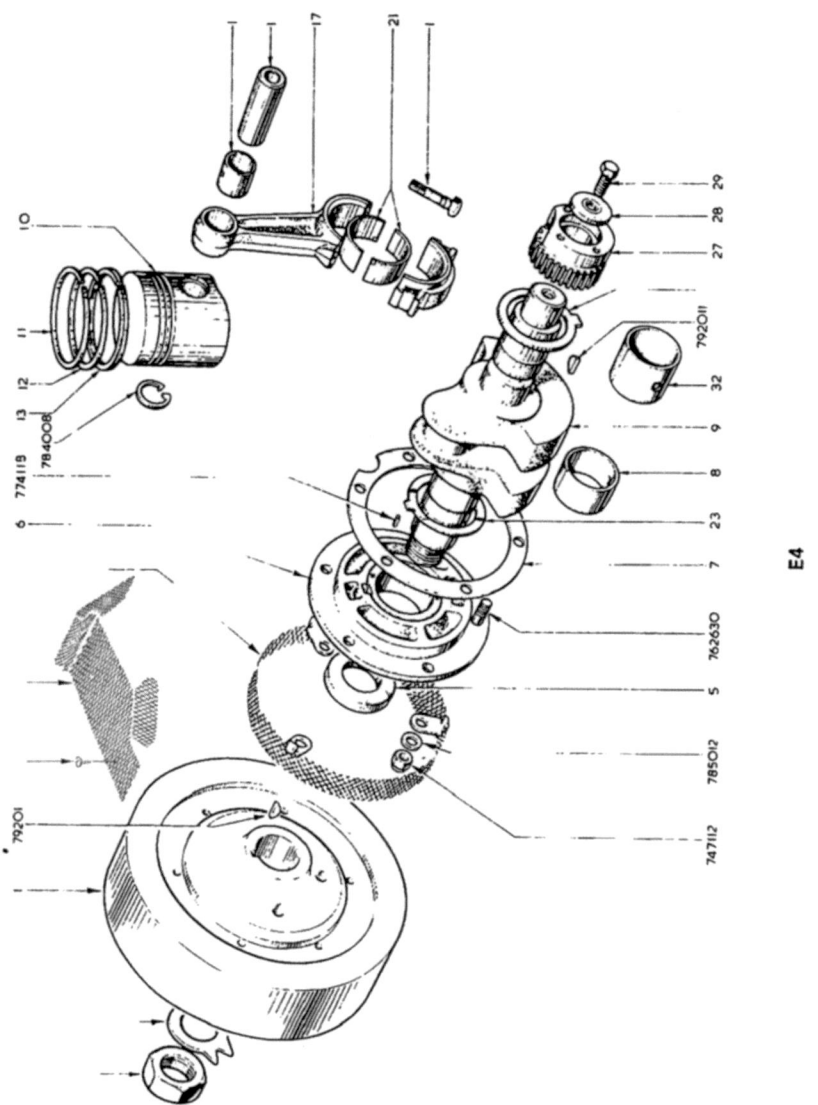

E4 CRANKSHAFT AND PISTON

Ref. No.	Description	AC1W
*WAC1a	Flywheel and Gear Ring (Electric Starting)	1
AAC5	Oil Seal	1
*ACC6	Housing — Main bearing (Flywheel end)	1
AAC7	Joint — Main Bearing Housing (Supplied only in Sets of Joints)	1
ACC8	Bearing — Main (Flywheel end) (Standard)	1
*ACC8−10	Bearing — Main (Flywheel end) (0.010" Undersize)	1
*ACC8−20	Bearing — Main (Flywheel end) (0.020" Undersize)	1
*ACC9	Crankshaft	1
*ACC10	Piston Assembly, complete with Rings, Pin and Circlips (Standard)	1
*ACC10 + 20	Piston Assembly, complete with Rings, Pin and Circlips (0.020" Oversize)	1
*ACC10 + 30	Piston Assembly, complete with Rings, Pin and Circlips (0.030" Oversize)	1
*ACC10 + 40	Piston Assembly, complete with Rings, Pin and Circlips (0.040" Oversize)	1
ABC11	Ring — Compression (Chromium Plated) (Standard)	
*ABC11 + 20	Ring — Compression (Chromium Plated) (0.020" Oversize)	1
*ABC11 + 30	Ring — Compression (Chromium Plated) (0.030" Oversize)	
*ABC11 + 40	Ring — Compression (Chromium Plated) (0.040" Oversize)	Only supplied in Standard or Oversize Sets
ABC12	Ring — Compression (Plain) (Standard)	1
*ABC12 + 20	Ring — Compression (Plain) (0.020" Oversize)	1
*ABC12 + 30	Ring — Compression (Plain) (0.030" Oversize)	1
*ABC12 + 40	Ring — Compression (Plain) (0.040" Oversize)	1
ABC13	Ring — Scraper (Standard)	
*ABC13 + 20	Ring — Scraper (0.020" Oversize)	1
*ABC13 + 30	Ring — Scraper (0.030" Oversize)	1
*ABC13 + 40	Ring — Scraper (0.040" Oversize)	1
ABC15	Gudgeon Pin	1
AAC16	Bush — Small End	1
*ACC17a	Connecting Rod Assembly, complete with Small End Bush, Standard Large End Bearing and Bolts	1
AAC18	Bolt — Large End	2
AAC21	Bearing — Large End (Standard)	1 pr.
*AAC21−10	Bearing — Large End (0.010" Undersize)	1 pr.
*AAC21−20	Bearing — Large End (0.020" Undersize)	1 pr.
AAC23	Washer — Crankshaft Thrust	2
AAC27	Gearwheel — Crankshaft	1
AAC28	Plate — Gearwheel Retaining	1
AAC29	Screw — Gearwheel Retaining	1
AAC32	Bearing — Main (Gear end) (Standard)	1
*AAC32−10	Bearing — Main (Gear end) (0.010" Undersize)	1
*AAC32−20	Bearing — Main (Gear end) (0.020" Undersize)	1
AAC84	Bolt — Flywheel Extension Shaft	4
AAC101	Tabwasher — Flywheel	1
AAC103	Nut — Flywheel	1
ACC281	Guard — Flywheel	1
WAC281	Guard — Flywheel	1
AAC284	Screw — Crankshaft Extension Shaft	4
AAC285	Oil Seal — Crankshaft Extension Shaft	1
WAC301	Screw — Flywheel Guard	1

*Indicates part not illustrated

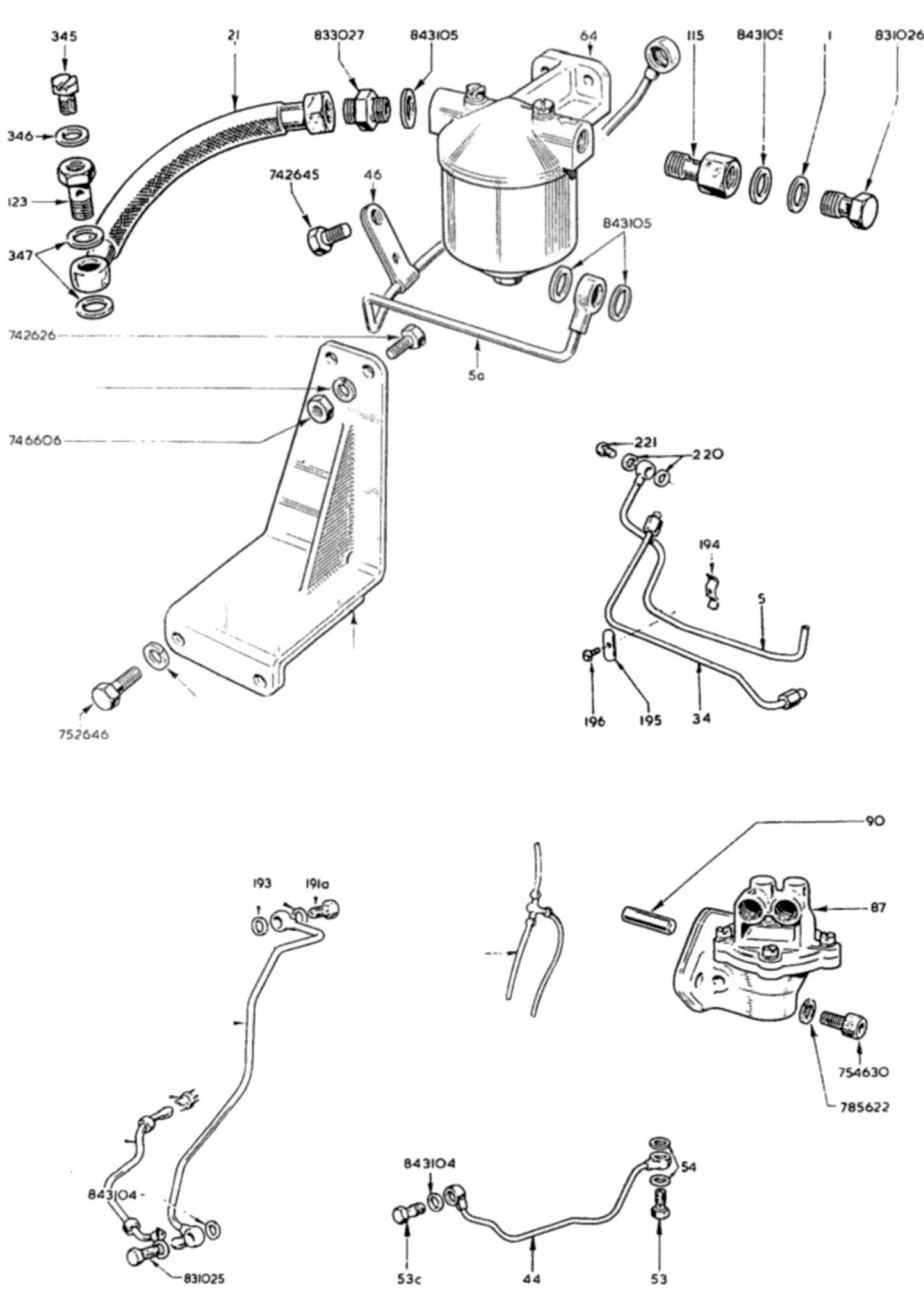

E5

E5　FUEL FILTER AND PIPES

Ref. No.	Description	AC1W
ACE1	Union — Main Bearing Housing (Flywheel end)	1
WAE5	Pipe — Injector Leak-off	1
ACE5a	Pipe — Injector Leak-off (Fuel Feed Pump)	1
WAE34	Pipe — Fuel (Pump to Injector)	1
ACE36	Bracket — Fuel Filter (Fuel Feed Pump)	1
ACE44	Pipe — Oil (Crankcase to Bearing Housing) (Gear end)	1
JE46	Clip—Leak-off Pipe (Fuel Feed Pump)	1
ACE53	Banjo Bolt — Bearing Housing	1
ZPE53c	Banjo Bolt — Crankcase (Bearing Housing Oil Pipe)	1
ACE54	Joint Washer — Bearing Housing Oil Pipe	2
ACE55	Pipe — Oil (Crankcase to Cylinder Head)	1
ASE64	Filter — Fuel (for use on engines having a 2 gal. Fuel Tank or a separately mounted Fuel Tank)	1
ACE67	Pipe — Oil (Crankcase to Main Bearing) (Flywheel end)	1
	†Pump — Fuel Feed	1
	†Push Rod — Fuel Feed Pump	1
CE115	Adaptor — Fuel Filter (Fuel Feed Pump)	1
	†Pipe — Fuel (Feed Pump to Filter) (Flexible)	1
ABE218	Pipe Assembly — Self-bleed	1
AAE123	Banjo Bolt — Fuel Pump (for use on engines having a separately mounted Fuel Tank)	1
ABE191a	Banjo Bolt — Cylinder Head	1
ABE193	Joint Washer — Cylinder Head	2
AAE194	Clip — Fuel Pipe	1
AAE195	Plate — Fuel Pipe Clip	1
AAE196	Screw — Fuel Pipe Clip	1
AAE220	Joint Washer — Injector Leak-off Pipe	2
AAE221	Banjo Bolt — Injector Leak-off Pipe	1
AAE345	Vent Screw — Fuel Pump (for use on engines having a separately mounted Fuel Tank)	1
AAE346	Washer — Vent Screw (for use on engines having a separately mounted Fuel Tank)	1
AAE347	Joint Washer — Fuel Pump (Supplied only in Sets of Joints)	2

†See General Assembly E15

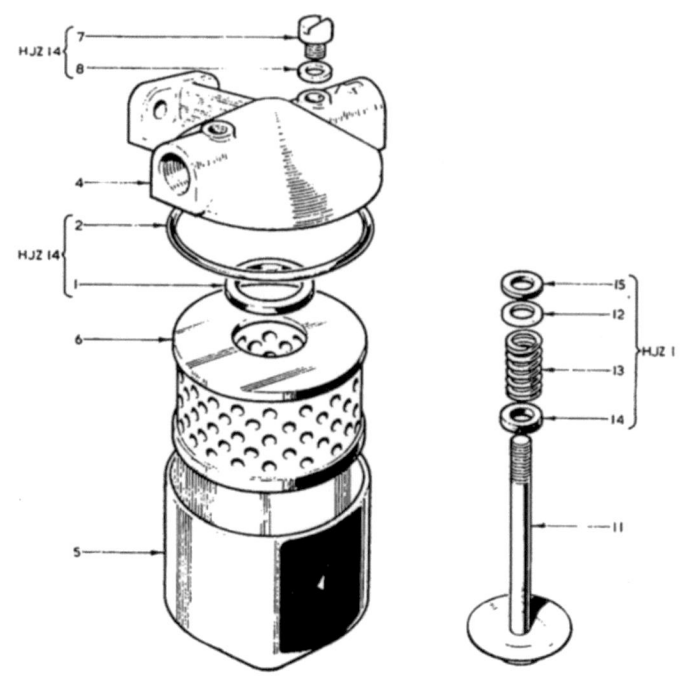

E6 FUEL FILTER ASE64

Ref. No.		Description
ASE64/4		Head
ASE64/5		Bowl
ASE64/6		Element
ASE64/11		Bolt – Centre
HJZ14	Spare Parts Pack, consisting of:	
	ASE64/1	Joint Washer – Element
	ASE64/2	Seal – Bowl
	ASE64/7	Screw – Vent
	ASE64/8	Washer – Vent Screw
	ASE64/12	Washer – Centre Bolt
	ASE64/13	Spring – Centre Bolt
	ASE64/14	Seal – Centre Bolt (Lower)
	ASE64/15	Seal – Centre Bolt (Upper)

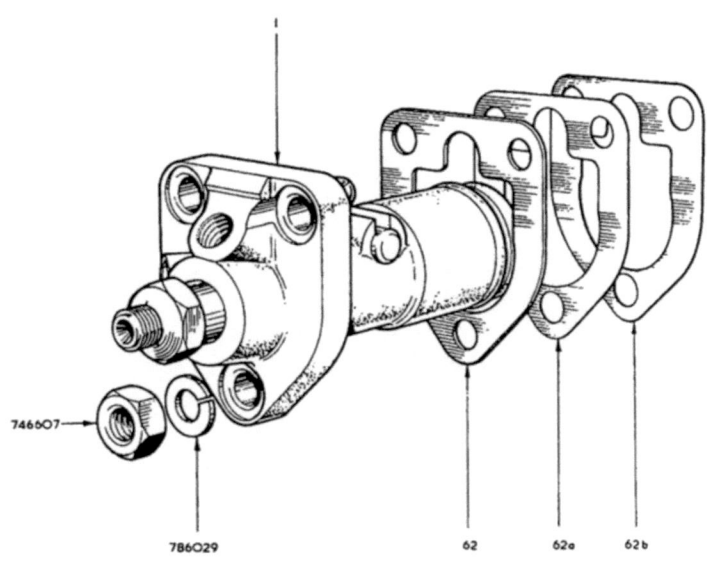

E7   FUEL PUMP

Ref. No.	Description	AC1W
AAN1	Pump – Fuel Injection (Fixed Speed and Two-speed up to 3000 rev/min) ...	1
ACN1	Pump – Fuel Injection (Fixed Speed and Two-speed – 3600 rev/min) ...	1
AAN62	Shim – Fuel Injection Pump (0.005") ...	As required
AAN62a	Shim – Fuel Injection Pump (0.0025")	As required
AAN62b	Shim – Fuel Injection Pump (0.025")	As required

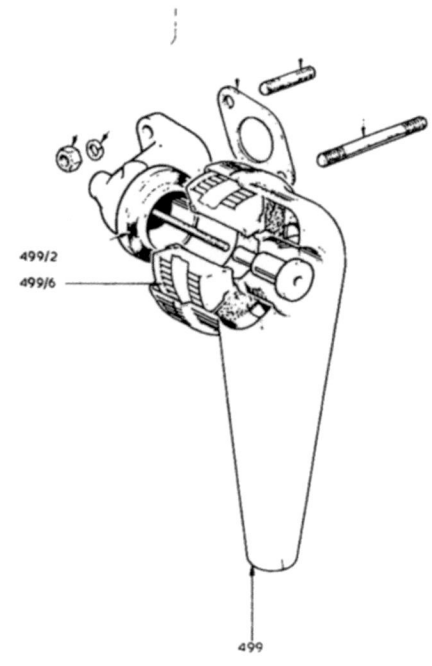

E8 AIR CLEANER

Ref. No.	Description	AC1W
AAF63	Joint – Air Inlet Manifold (Supplied only in Sets of Joints)	1
ACF499	Air Cleaner, complete with Manifold, Seal and Element	1
AAF499/2	Seal – Air Cleaner (Casing to Manifold)	1
AAF499/6	Element – Air Cleaner	1

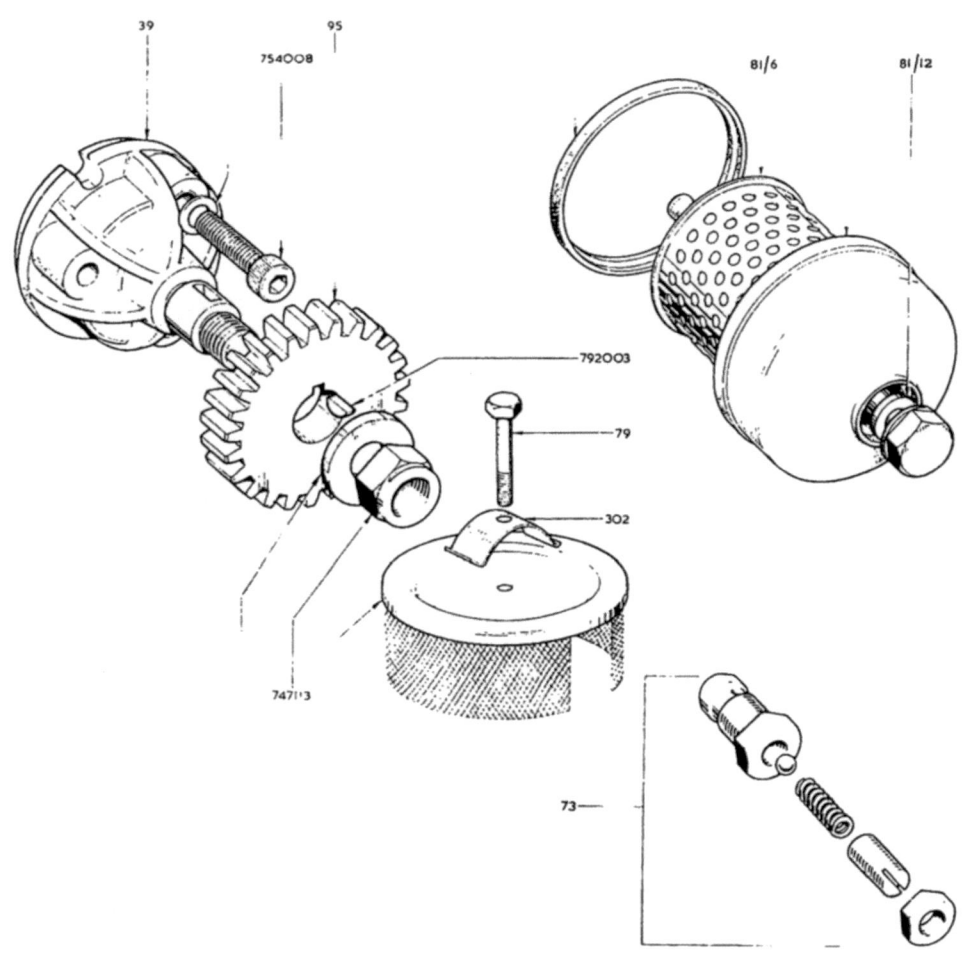

E9 OIL PUMP, OIL FILTER AND STRAINER

Ref. No.	Description	AC1W
AAK39	Pump — Lubricating Oil	1
ABK73	Relief Valve Assembly	1
AAK78	Strainer — Oil Pump	1
AAK79	Bolt — Oil Pump Strainer ...	1
AAK81	Filter — Lubricating Oil, complete with Joint and Element	1
AAK81/6	Element — Filter ...	1
AAK81/12	Joint Washer — Filter Centre Bolt	1
AAK82	Joint Washer — Filter	1
AAK95	Gearwheel — Oil Pump	1
AAK302	Clip — Oil Pump Strainer	1

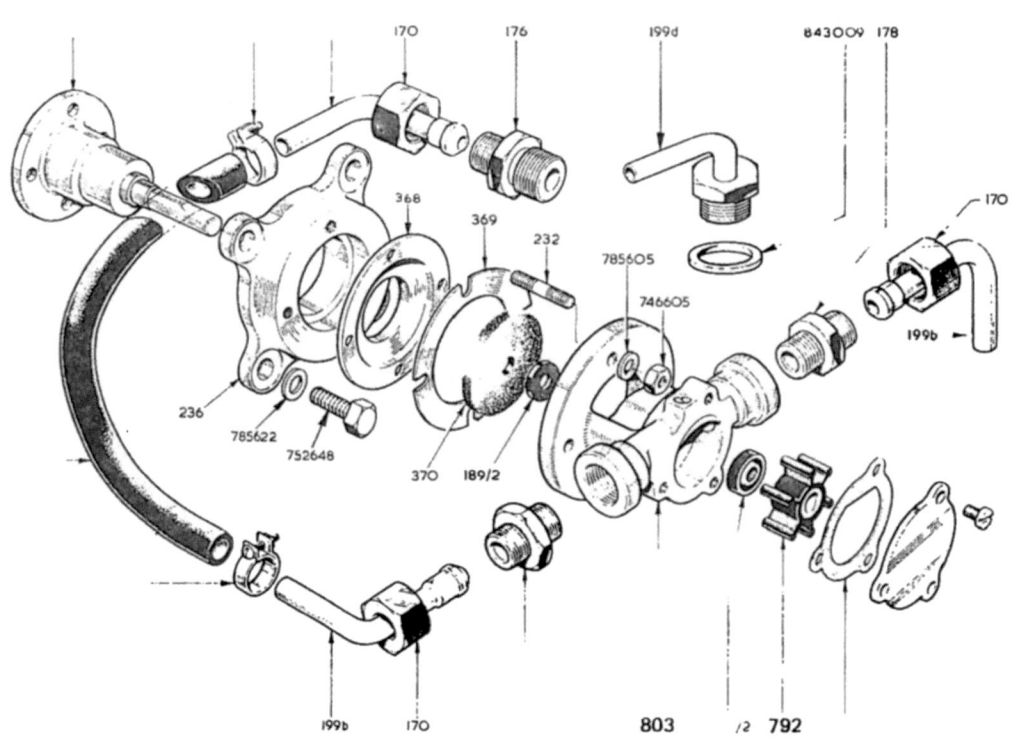

E10 WATER PUMP

Ref. No.	Description	AC1W
WAK170	Nut – Union ...	3
WAK176	Union – Cylinder	1
WAK178	Union – Water Pump	2
403 GM 803	Pump – Water	1
WAK189/2	Seal – Water Pump	1 pr.
403 GM 792	Impeller – Water Pump	1
WAK189/15	Joint – Water Pump Cover	1
WAK199b	Pipe Assembly – Hose Connector	3
WAK199d	Pipe Assembly – Cylinder Head ...	1
WAK199g	Hose – Water (Pump to Cylinder)	1
WAK218	Shaft – Water Pump (for use on engines without Raised Hand Starting)	1
WAK232	Stud – Water Pump	4
WAK236	Housing – Water Pump (for use on engines without Raised Hand Starting)	1
WAK368	Plate – Adaptor (Water Pump)	1
WAK369	Shim – Water Pump Adaptor ...	As required
WAK370	Sealing Washer – Water Pump Shaft	1
WAK371	Clip – Hose	2

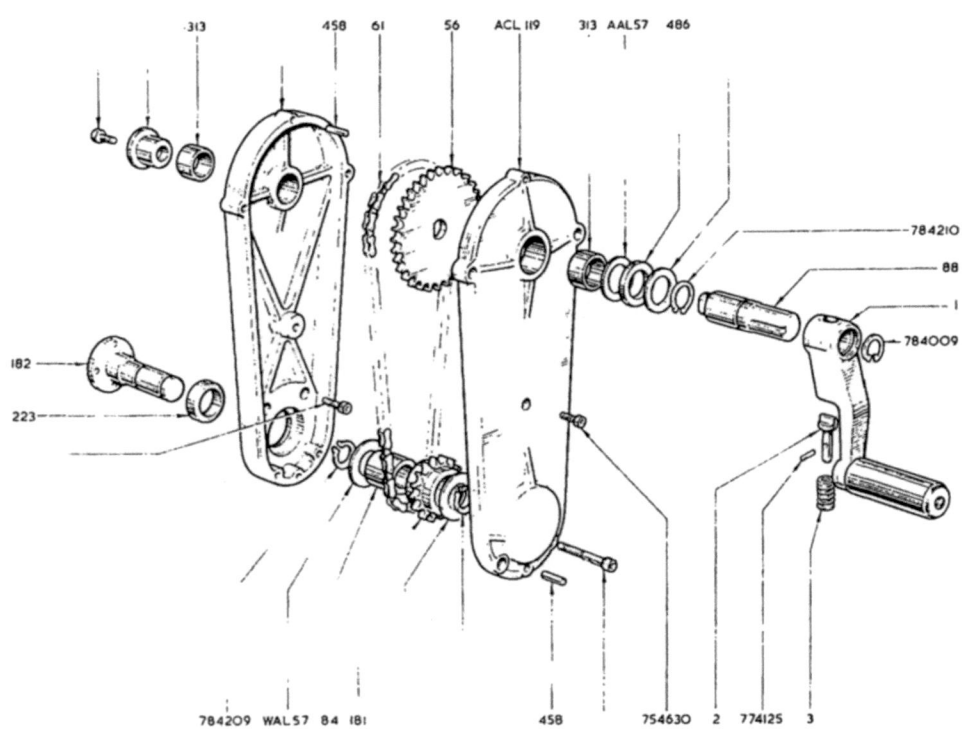

E11 RAISED HAND STARTING

Ref. No.	Description	AC1W
WAL1	Starting Handle Assembly, consisting of:	
AAL2	Plunger – Starting Handle	1
AAL3	Spring – Starting Handle Plunger	1
774125	Pin – Starting Handle Plunger	1
784009	Circlip – Starting Handle	1
WAL56	Chainwheel – Upper	1
AAL57	Washer – Starting Shaft	2
WAL57	Washer – Clutch	2
WAL61	Chain – Starting	1
AAL68	Shaft – Chainwheel Retaining	1
AAL83	Screw – Retaining Shaft	1
WAL84	Clutch – Roller	1
WAL88	Shaft – Starting Handle	1
ACL119	Housing – Chain (Outer)	1
WAL119	Housing – Chain (Inner)	1
WAL119a	Housing – Chain (Outer) (for use with Water Pump)	1
WAL181	Chainwheel – Lower	1
ACL182	Shaft – Camshaft Extension	1
WAL182	Shaft – Camshaft Extension (for use with Water Pump)	1
AAL223	Sleeve – Spigot	1
AAL313	Bush – Chain Housing	2
AAL458	Dowel – Chain Housing	2
WAL486	Washer – Starting Handle Shaft	1

E12 AIR CLEANER, FUEL & OIL FILTER ELEMENT PACKS

Ref. No.	Description		AC1W
ACZ12	Element Pack – Air Cleaner		1
	Consisting of:		
	ACF499/6	Element – Air Filter	4
AAZ9a	Complete Set of Element Packs		1
	Consisting of:		
	AAZ10	Element Pack – Fuel Filter	1
	AAZ11	Element Pack – Oil Filter	1
	ACZ12	Element Pack – Air Cleaner	1
AAZ10	Element Pack – Fuel Filter		1
	Consisting of:		
	AAE24	Joint Washer – Element Plug	2
	AAE28	Element – Fuel Filter	2
AAZ11	Element Pack – Oil Filter		1
	Consisting of:		
	AAK81/6	Element – Oil Filter	8
	AAK81/12	Joint Washer	8
ACZ2b	Decarbonising Set of Joints		1
	Consisting of: (See Plates B and F)		
	AAB4	Joint – Rocker Box Cover	1
	ACB58	Gasket – Cylinder Head	1
	ACB61a	Washer – Nozzle Shield	1
	AAF50	Gasket – Exhaust	1
	AAF63	Joint – Air Inlet Manifold	1
AAZ3	Conversion Set of Joints		1
	Consisting of: (See Plates A, C, D and E)		
	AAA56	Joint – Gear Cover	1
	AAA139	Joint – Sump	1
	AAC7	Joint – Main Bearing Housing	1
	AAD256	Joint – Cover	1
	AAE347	Joint Washer – Fuel Pump	1
	843105	Joint Washer ½" (Copper)	1
ACZ1b	Complete Set of Joi		1
	Consisting of:		
	ACZ2b	Decarbonising Set of Joints	1
	AAZ3	Conversion Set of Joints	1

E13 SPEEDER SPRING DETAILS

Ref. No.	Colour	Position	Engine Speed	AC1W
AAD125g	Aluminium/Yellow	Bands	1500	1
AAD125e	Blue/Orange	Ends	1800	1
AAD125e	Blue/Orange	Ends	2100	1
AAD125d	Aluminium/Brown	Ends	2500	1
AAD125d	Aluminium/Brown	Ends	3000	1
†AAD125	Blue/Orange	Bands	3600	1
†AAD125a	Aluminium/Blue	Bands	Variable and Two-speed	1

For AC1W 3600 rev/min fixed speed engines fuel pump ACN1 must be fitted.

E14 COMMON DETAIL PARTS – AC1W

†Denotes that part must be obtained from G & M P.P. or their agents
Stud lengths quoted are overall lengths

Ref. No.	Description
702223	Screw – Hex Head, M6 x 12mm (Plated)
702225	Screw – Hex Head, M6 x 16mm (Plated)
706104	Nut, M6 (Plated)
714103	Grubscrew – Socket Head, 2BA x ¼" (Cup Point)
742047	Screw – Hex Head, 5/16" UNF x ¾"
742624	Screw – Hex Head, ¼" UNF x 5/8" (Plated)
742625	Screw – Hex Head, ¼" UNF x ¾" (Plated)
742626	Screw – Hex Head, ¼" UNF x 7/8" (Plated)
742643	Screw – Hex Head, ¼" UNF x 5½" (Plated)
742645	Screw – Hex Head, 5/16" UNF x ½" (Plated)
742647	Screw – Hex Head, 5/16" UNF x ¾" (Plated)
742649	Screw – Hex Head, 5/16" UNF x 1" (Plated)
744002	Capscrew – Socket Head, ¼" UNF x ½"
744003	Capscrew – Socket Head, ¼" UNF x 5/8"
744030	Capscrew – Socket Head, 5/16" UNF x ¾"
744238	Grubscrew – Socket Head, 7/16" UNF x ½" (Cup Point)
744602	Capscrew – Socket Head, ¼" UNF x ½" (Plated)
745030	Bolt – Hex Head, 5/16" UNF x 1 3/8"
746006	Nut, ¼" UNF
746007	Nut, 5/16" UNF
746016	Locknut, ¼" UNF
†746026	Nut
746605	Nut, 10 – 32 UNF (Plated)
746606	Nut, ¼" UNF (Plated)
746607	Nut, 5/16" UNF (Plated)
746616	Locknut, ¼" UNF (Plated)
747017	Nut, 5/16" UNF (Self-locking) (Nylon Insert) (Thin)
747029	Nut, 10 – 32 UNF (Self-locking) (Nylon Insert) (Plated)
747112	Nut, 5/16"UNF (Self-locking) (Phosphated) (Thin)
747113	Nut, 3/8" UNF (Self-locking) (Phosphated) (Thin)
747115	Nut, ½" UNF (Self-locking) (Phosphated) (Thin)
748003	Wingnut, ¼" UNF (Plated)
752024	Screw – Hex Head, ¼" UNC x 5/8"
752625	Screw – Hex Head, ¼" UNC x ¾" (Plated)
752645	Screw – Hex Head, 5/16" UNC x ½" (Plated)
752646	Screw – Hex Head, 5/16" UNC x 5/8" (Plated)
752648	Screw – Hex Head, 5/16" UNC x 7/8" (Plated)
752649	Screw – Hex Head, 5/16" UNC x 1" (Plated)
752653	Screw – Hex Head, 5/16" UNC x 1½" (Plated)
752669	Screw – Hex Head, 3" UNC x ¾" (Plated)
752670	Screw – Hex Head, -" UNC x 7/8" (Plated)
752672	Screw – Hex Head, /8" UNC x 1 1/8" (Plated)
754003	Capscrew – Socket Head, ¼" UNC x 5/8"
754004	Capscrew – Socket Head, ¼" UNC x ¾"
754005	Capscrew – Socket Head, ¼" UNC x 7/8"
754008	Capscrew – Socket Head, ¼" UNC x 1½"
754032	Capscrew – Socket Head, 5/16" UNC x 1"
754058	Capscrew – Socket Head, 3/8" UNC x 1"
754203	Grubscrew – Socket Head, ¼" UNC x 3/8" (Cup Point)
754604	Capscrew – Socket Head, ¼" UNC x ¾" (Plated)
654605	Capscrew – Socket Head, ¼" UNC x 7/8" (Plated)
754630	Capscrew – Socket Head, 5/16" UNC x ¾" (Plated)
754632	Capscrew – Socket Head, 5/16" UNC x 1" (Plated)
754637	Capscrew – Socket Head, 5/16" UNC x 2¼" (Plated)
754658	Capscrew – Socket Head, 3/8" UNC x 1" (Plated)
754784	Capscrew – Socket Head, ¼" UNC x 1 1/8" (Plated)

761001	Stud, ¼" UNF x 1"
762037	Stud, 5/16" UNF/UNC x 2 1/8"
762629	Stud, 5/16" UNF/UNC x 1 1/8" (Plated)
762630	Stud, 5/16" UNF/UNC x 1¼" (Plated)
762632	Stud, 5/16" UNF/UNC x 1½" (Plated)
762636	Stud, 5/16" UNF/UNC x 2" (Plated)
762645	Stud, 5/16" UNF/UNC x 3 1/8" (Plated)
763404	Screw – Pan Head, No. 4 x 3/8" (Self-tapping) (Plated)
763832	Screw – Hammer Drive, No. 10 x 3/8" (Plated)
773148	Split Pin, 3/64" x 3/8"
773601	Split Pin, 1/16" x 3/8" (Plated)
774107	Pin – Spring Tension, 3/32" x 5/8" (Plated)
774118	Pin – Spring Tension, 1/8" x ¼" (Plated)
774122	Pin – Spring Tension, 1/8" x ½" (Plated)
774125	Pin – Spring Tension, 1/8" x ¾" (Plated)
774160	Pin – Spring Tension, 3/16" x 7/8" (Plated)
774161	Pin – Spring Tension, 3/16" x 1" (Plated)
774204	Pin – Spring Tension, 1/8" x 11/16" (Plated)
774205	Pin – Spring Tension, 3/16" x 11/16" (Plated)
774213	Pin – Spring Tension, 1/16" x ¼" (Plated)
784008	Circlip, 7/8" (Internal)
784009	Circlip, 1" (Internal)
784203	Circlip, 3/8" (External)
784205	Circlip, 9/16" (External)
784209	Circlip, 1" (External)
784210	Circlip, 1 1/8" (External)
785011	Washer – Bright, ¼" (Small) (Heavy Gauge)
785012	Washer – Bright, 5/16" (Small) (Heavy Gauge)
785512	Washer – Bright, 6mm (Plated)
785605	Washer, 2BA (Small) (Heavy Gauge) (Plated)
785611	Washer, ¼" (Small) (Heavy Gauge) (Plated)
785612	Washer, 5/16" (Small) (Heavy Gauge) (Plated)
785613	Washer, 3/8" (Small) (Heavy Gauge) (Plated)
785621	Washer, ¼" (Small) (Light Gauge) (Plated)
785622	Washer, 5/16" (Small) (Light Gauge) (Plated)
785642	Washer, ¼" (Large) (Light Gauge) (Plated)
786028	Spring Washer – Single Coil, ¼" (Rectangular Section)
786029	Spring Washer – Single Coil, 5/16" (Rectangular Section)
786078	Spring Washer – Single Coil, ¼" (Rectangular Section) (Plated)
786079	Spring Washer – Single Coil, 5/16" (Rectangular Section) (Plated)
786710	Washer – Shakeproof, 5/8" (Internal Teeth) (Sealing)
790183	Key – Parallel, ¼" x ¼" x 1 3/8" (Round End)
792002	Key – Woodruff, 3/32" x 3/8"
792003	Key – Woodruff, 1/8" x 3/8"
792007	Key – Woodruff, 3/32" x 5/8"
792009	Key – Woodruff, 5/32" x 5/8"
792011	Key – Woodruff, 5/32" x ¾"
792018	Key – Woodruff, 5/16" x 1"
†821530	Elbow – 90° (Male) (Copper) (Pipe fitting one end only)
831025	Bolt – Banjo, 1/8" BSP (Plated)
831026	Bolt – Banjo, ¼" BSP
†833027	Union (Pipe fitting one end only)
836007	Bush – Reducing, ¾" x ½" BSP
843005	Joint Washer, ½" (Fibre)
843007	Joint Washer, ¾" (Fibre)
843009	Joint Washer, 1" (Fibre)
843104	Joint Washer, 3/8" (Copper)
843105	Joint Washer, ½" (Copper)
†844105	Oil Seal, No.10
†844106	Oil Seal, No.11

E15 GENERAL ASSEMBLY

	Petter AC1W Engine	1
	Markon Alternator LCC.19C	1
252/GM.1011	Fuel Lift Pump Kit	1
200/GM.1477	Drip Tray	1
201/GM.683	Anti-Vibration Mount	4
201/GM.A373/3	Anti-Vibration Mount Cover	4
202/GM.1354	Rear Mounting Bar	1
202/GM.1352	Front Mounting Bar	1
202/GM.1411	Mounting Stud	1
205/GM.1117	Sump Drain Extension Tube	1
250/GM.301	Worm Drive Clip	4
203/GM.1261	Water Injection Elbow	1
251/GM.361	¼" B.S.P. Nipple	1
251/GM.363	¼" B.S.P. M/F Elbow	1
251/GM.1145	Male Coupling ¼"/⅜" B.S.P.	1
259/GM.1345	⅜" O.D. Stainless Pipe x 3" LG	1
259/GM.1346	⅜" O.D. Black Plastic Hose x 25"	1
151/GM.360	Oil Pressure Switch	1
825001	⅛" B.S.P. Socket	1
833025	⅛" B.S.P. Union	1
843104	Joint	1
150/GM.1476	Control Box Assembly	1
151/GM.270	Start Button	1
153/GM.A124/7	Ammeter ± 15 amps	1
152/GM.211	Fuel Solenoid Relay	1
156/GM.400	Terminal Stud Red	1
156/GM.401	Terminal Stud Black	1
155/GM.107	Capacitor	2
151/GM.357	Stop Button	1
151/GM.365	Key Switch	1
151/GM.368	Barrel Lock and Key	1
156/GM.A339/1	Terminal Block 3 way 30 amp.	1
156/GM.A339/15	Terminal Block 3 way 15 amp.	1
156/GM.A339/7	Terminal Block 7 way	1
163/GM.504	¾" Dia. Rubber Grommet	1
163/GM.299	Terry Clip 1½"	4
163/GM.500	Grommet	4
452/GM.1377	Spacer	4
402/GM.152	Starter Motor	1
252/GM.1007	A.C. Fuel Pump	1
250/GM.1119	Fuel Pipe	1
252/GM.1009	Push Rod	1
252/GM.1010	Banjo Bolt	2
250/GM.1120	Banjo Union	1
250/GM.1112	Copper Washer	4
List 73B	Fuel Solenoid	1
160/GM.111	Lamp Holder Red	1
160/GM.112	Lamp Midget Flange	1

SECTION F

LCC and LCS Alternators

F1	GENERAL DESCRIPTION
F2	SERVICING NOTE – WARNING
F3	SERVICING
F4	INSTALLATION AND VOLTAGE TESTING
F5	NO VOLTAGE CHECK
F6	REMOVING THE GENERATOR
F7	REFITTING THE GENERATOR
F8	WIRING DIAGRAM

MARKON TYPE LC ALTERNATOR

F1–1 GENERAL DESCRIPTION

Markon LC alternators are a simple type of rotating armature machine and incorporate a static, self regulating, self exciting, power factor compensating control unit.

They are designed for 50 or 60 cycles output at a speed of 3000 or 3600 r.p.m. Voltage regulati the order of $\pm$ 5% from no load to full load allowing for standard engine governing.

The voltage regulation system employed in these alternators is of the current compounding type. At no load the excitation current is obtained from a silicon rectifier connected across one pair of output lines and condensers in series with the supply to the rectifier limit the current to the required value. A small amount of adjustment to this current is obtained by means of a preset resistor in parallel with the field.

With increase in load, additional excitation current is obtained from the current transformer. The secondary output current which is proportional to the primary or load current is added vectorially, by parallel connections, to the no load excitation current. This then gives the required excitation even under conditions of lagging power factor loads.

No external voltage trimmer is required.

The output volts are set during works test and unless there is any marked difference in engine speed it should not normally be necessary to alter the voltage setting. If necessary the no load voltage may be adjusted slightly by means of the resistor fitted in the non drive end bracket. It should be noted however, that the no load voltage will rise after load has been applied the first time after starting the set.

BRUSHES:

Grade M4 or equivalent
Part No. 010-001

Bearing Part No. 014–001

F2–1 SERVICING NOTE – WARNING

The rectifier plate is attached by a single fixing between two of the webs of the bearing support bracket, and it is possible when the enclosing cover is removed for the plate to be deflected sufficiently to cause a short circuit. When replacing the enclosing cover at any time, check that the plate is always positioned square with the axis of the generator and ensure that this position is not altered during the replacement.

The plate cannot be deflected if it is correctly positioned and the enclosing cover fitted.

Do not run the generator with the enclosing cover removed. This will upset the flow of cooling air through the generator and also expose the rectifier plate to possible deflection.

When refitting the louvered end plate, ensure that the air intake guide slats incline downwards and outwards from the generator.

F3–1 SERVICING EVERY 100 HOURS

(a) Check that the brushes are central on the slip rings. Renew worn or damaged brushes.
(b) Clean the surface of the slip rings. Do not use an abrasive. If slip rings are damaged the armature should be removed and the slip rings skimmed and polished.
(c) Use a compressed air jet to blow any dust out of the generator.
(d) The single bearing in the non drive end is sealed and requires no lubrication.
(e) Examine cables in the control box and generator for damage, and tightness of connection.

F4–1 INSULATION RESISTANCE AND HIGH VOLTAGE FLASH TESTING

If it is necessary to carry out either of these tests it is important to disconnect radi interference suppression condensers if fitted, and to short circuit silicon diodes.

F5–1 NO OUTPUT

If when the load is applied the voltage fails to build up, check the serviceability of the capacitors situated in the control box.

F6—1 REMOVING THE GENERATOR

Detach the generator from its mounting to the carrying frame or drip tray, and with the engine mounting bolts still in position, slightly raise the generator and support the plant with a suitable block of wood placed underneath the engine flywheel housing.

Disconnect the starter cables between the engine and the control box on electric start models only, no other cables need be disconnected as the stator and control box can be removed as a complete unit.

Remove the enclosing cover and the louvre end plate, lift the brushes and secure them in a position clear of the slip rings. Brushes falling between the slip rings when the generator is being withdrawn may be damaged.

Remove the nut from the armature through stud and the eight flange bolts attaching the generator to the engine and carefully lift the stator and the control box clear of the engine.

To remove the armature it may be necessary to first break the hold between the armature and the stub shaft. Wrap the armature in suitable protective padding and apply a light blow with either a rubber mallet or a hide faced hammer. Do not hit the slip rings.

F7—1 REFITTING THE GENERATOR

The generator may be replaced either as a complete unit or the armature may be fitted first and the stator fitted over the armature. It is important that extreme care be exercised during refitting to ensure that the brushes are not damaged.

When the generator has been positioned, tighten the flange to engine attachment bolts, the generator mounting bolts and the armature shaft securing nut. Reconnect any electrical cables previously disconnected and check that all brushes are positioned centrally on the slip rings.

Replace the enclosing cover and the end plate louvre.

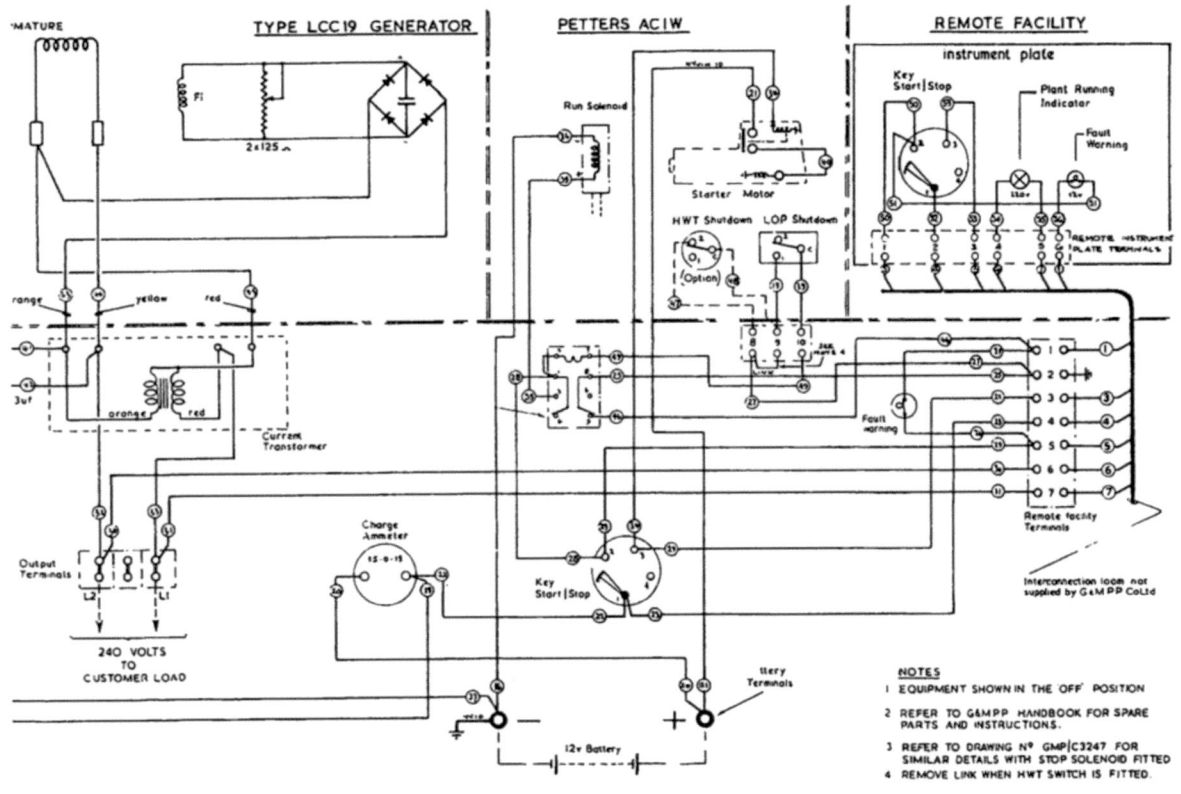

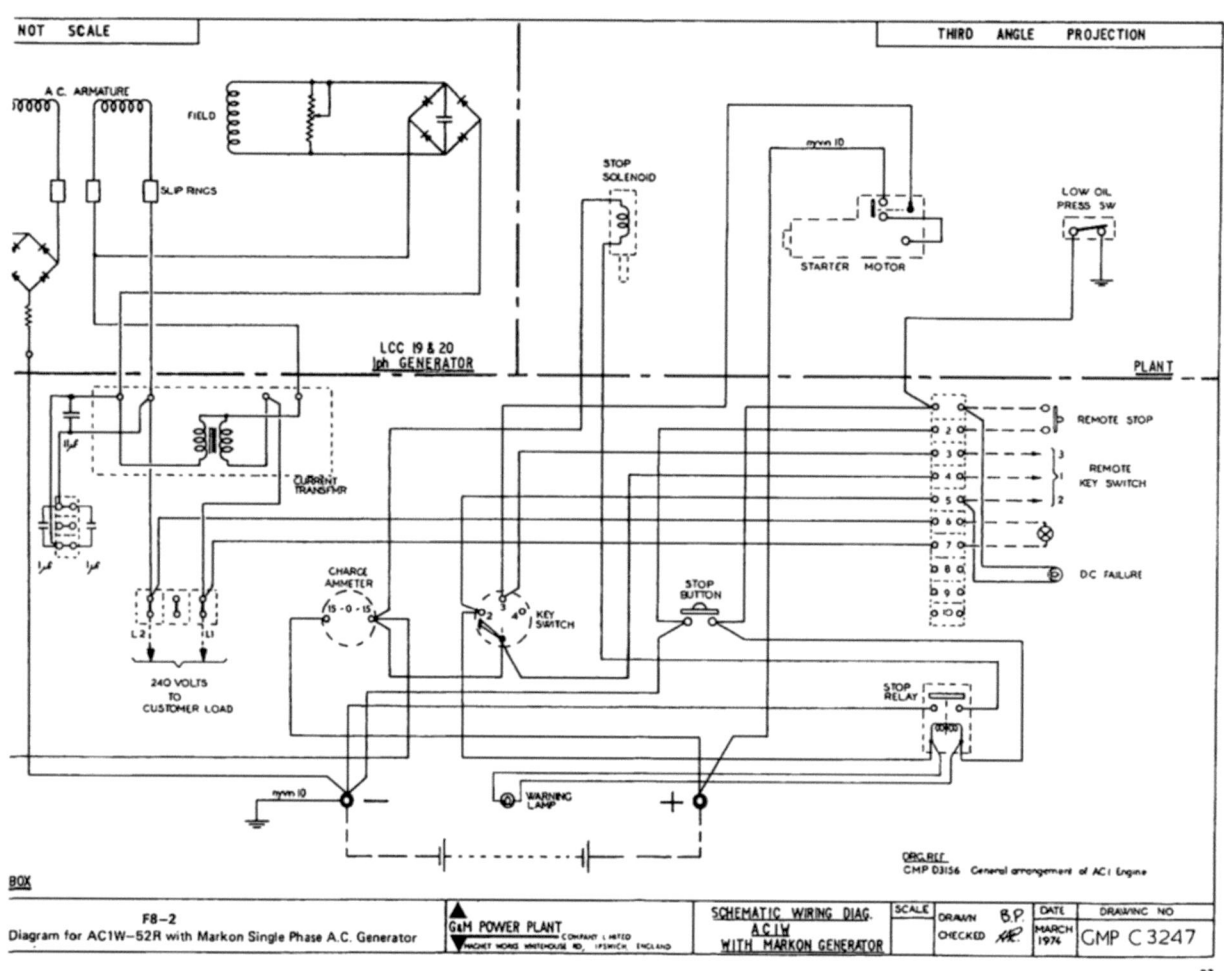

SECTION G
RN 4050 ALTERNATOR

G1	SPECIFICATION
G2	SAFETY NOTE
G3	DESCRIPTION
G4	REMOVAL AND REPLACEMENT
G5	SERVICING
G6	LIST OF PART NUMBERS
G7	WIRING DIAGRAM

G1   4AC1W–53R WITH RN4050 A.C. GENERATOR
       SPECIFICATION:–
       3 KW MARINE GENERATING SET.
       SINGLE PHASE – 120/240 VOLT CONNECTIONS 50 HZ. OUTPUT
       12 VOLT CONTROL CIRCUIT NEGATIVE EARTH RETURN.
       12 VOLT ELECTRIC START WITH REMOTE FACILITY.
       12 VOLT BATTERY CHARGING – TAPPING FROM ARMATURE WINDINGS.
       LOW OIL PRESSURE CUT OUT SWITCH.
       STOP RELAY.

G2   SAFETY NOTE:
       BEFORE CARRYING OUT PERIODIC SERVICING OR ANY REPAIR WHICH NECESSITATES THE REMOVAL OF ANY ENGINE OR ELECTRICAL COMPONENT OR WHICH REQUIRES OIL DRAINING OR COOLING WATER DISCONNECTION, ALWAYS DISCONNECT THE STARTER BATTERY.

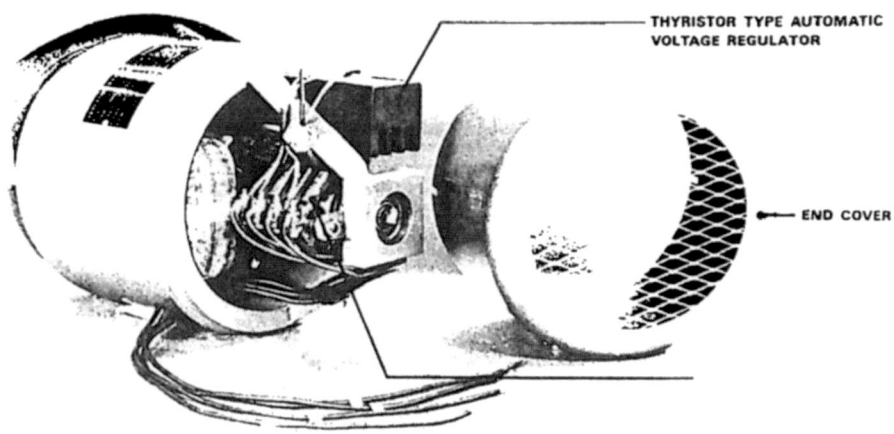

RN4050 A.C. GENERATOR
Fig. 1G

G3   A.C. GENERATOR TYPE RN.4050
DESCRIPTION

The 'RN' range of high performance, self exciting alternators have been specifically designed for close coupling to high speed petrol, propane and diesel engines conforming to SAE standards.

The rotor has a female taper for direct mounting on to the engine shaft and is secured by a through bolt.

The stator frame is arranged for bolting directly on to the engine crank case. Additional support for the rotor is provided by a bearing at the non-drive end of the machine.

The field system (2 poles) is stationary in the stator frame and is supplied with power by a thyristor type automatic voltage regulator mounted within the machine.

AC power from the rotor is taken via adequately rated sliprings and brushgear.

Rotor.
Laminations of high grade electrical steel are pressed on to the precision machined steel shaft. Dual wound AC windings are securely held in fully insulated slots and connected to four sliprings which are of moulded construction.

The shaft also carries a radial type fan to give adequate cooling. This being located at the drive end of the machine.

Stator.
The stator housing is made from high quality drawn steel tube and carries the non-drive end bracket complete with bearing and the drive end bracket which is spigotted to SAE standards for engine mounting. Both end brackets are cast iron.

The non-drive end bracket carries the automatic voltage regulator which can easily be removed.

RATING
The machines are continuously rated in accordance with BSS 2613 dated 1970. Full KVA output at 0.8 power factor being available with the AC windings connected in series. (nominal voltage 230 volts).

INSULATION
Class 'F' Impregnated for use in tropical climates.

OUTPUT VOLTAGE
This is preset at the nominal value of 230 volts with provision for a ± 10% trim adjustment on the automatic voltage regulator.

AUTOMATIC VOLTAGE REGULATOR
This is positioned directly within the air inlet to the machine. It is encapsulated to protect against severe vibration and ingress of dirt. The performance of this regulator is exceptional giving a regulation better than ± 2½% from no load to full load for power factors from 0.8 to 1.0 including engine speed rise of up to 6%. For power factors between 0.8 and zero there is only a marginal reduction in the nominal KVA rating of the machine (related to 0.8 power factor).

REMOVAL AND REPLACEMENT.

TO REMOVE
(a) Disconnect the starter battery on plants with electric starting.
(b) Remove the control box lid and disconnect the leads to the engine and the output leads from the generator. Mark the leads to ensure correct re-connection.
(c) Remove the nut from the bottom of the generator support stud and place wood packing under the engine sump to provide support when the generator is removed.
(d) Remove the generator end cover, and the nut from the through bolt.
(e) Lift the brushes clear of the slip rings and secure them in a position so they cannot fall between the slip rings and become damaged when the generator is being withdrawn from the engine.
(f) Remove the four bolts securing the stator to the mounting flange and ease the generator away from the engine.
N.B. The grip between the tapered drive shaft and the armature may be too positive to allow the armature to be removed with the stator. To break the grip after the stator has been removed apply a light blow to the rim of the end bearing with a hide faced hammer.

TO REPLACE
(a) Ensure that the contacting faces of the tapered drive shaft and the armature internal taper are perfectly clean and then apply a thin film of grease.
(b) Slide the armature over the through bolt and fully engage the armature on the tapered drive shaft.
(c) Secure the brushes so that they will not foul the slip rings and carefully position the stator over the armature, locate the end bearing in the bearing housing and bolt the stator to the mounting flange.
(d) Remove the support packing from under the engine sump, position the generator support stud, refit and tighten the support stud nut.

78

(e) Refit and tighten the through stud nut, check that the slip rings are perfectly clean and positi the brushes centrally on the slip rings.
(f) Turn the engine very slowly by hand to check that there is no mechanical interference between the armature and the stator.
(g) Reconnect all cables previously disconnected in the control box, check all connections for tightness and all attachments for security. Refit the generator end cover.

G5 SERVICING

EVERY 100 HOURS

With the end cover removed:—
(a) Check that the brushes are central on the slip rings. Replace worn or damaged brushes.
(b) Blow out dust with a compressed air jet.
(c) Clean the slip rings with a clean cloth moistened with petrol or carbon tetrachloride.
Very fine sand paper may be used for cleaning slip rings. EMERY CLOTH MUST NOT BE USED.

VOLTAGE REGULATOR

This unit is preset and sealed and requires no servicing.

G6 LIST OF PART NUMBERS

Part Number	Description	Qty
AC1W	DIESEL ENGINE	1
ACA.248	FLYWHEEL COVER PLATE	1
RN.4050	ALTERNATOR C/W DRIVE SHAFT AND THROUGH BOLT	1
200GM.1477	DRIP TRAY	1
201GM.683	ANTI VIBRATION MOUNT	4
201GM.A373/3	ANTI VIBRATION MOUNT COVER	4
202GM.1352	FRONT MOUNTING BAR	1
202GM.1354	REAR MOUNTING BAR	1
202GM.1450	GENERATOR MOUNTING STUD	1
203GM.1261	WATER INJECTION ELBOW	1
250GM.1117	SUMP DRAIN EXTENSION TUBE	1
250GM.301	WORM DRIVE CLIP	4
251GM.361	¼" B.S.P. NIPPLE	1
251GM.363	¼" B.S.P.M/F ELBOW	1
251GM.1145	MALE COUPLING ¼"/⅜" B.S.P.	1
259GM.1345	⅜" O.D. x ⅜" L.G. STAINLESS PIPE	1
259GM.1346	⅜" O.D. BLACK PLASTIC HOSE x 25" L.G.	1
151GM.360	OIL PRESSURE SWITCH	1
825001	⅛" B.S.P. SOCKET	1
833025	⅛" B.S.P. UNION	1
843104	JOINT	1
150GM.1521	CONTROL BOX	1
150GM.1450	SIDE PLATE	1
150GM.1383	CONTROL BOX LID	1
151GM.270	START BUTTON	1
151GM.357	STOP BUTTON	1
151GM.365	KEY SWITCH	1
151GM.368	BARREL LOCK AND KEY	1
152GM.211	STOP RELAY	1
153GM.A124/7	AMMETER 15—0—15	1
154GM.233	RESISTOR 4 OHM	1
156GM.A339/1	TERMINAL BLOCK 3 WAY 30 AMP	1
156GM.A339/7	TERMINAL BLOCK 7 WAY	1

79

156GM.400	TERMINAL STUD RED	1
156GM.401	TERMINAL STUD BLACK	1
160GM.100	NEON INDICATOR	1
160GM.111	LAMP HOLDER RED	1
160GM.112	LAMP MIDGET FLANGE	1
163GM.504	GROMMET RUBBER	2
164GM.914	BRIDGE RECTIFIER	1
252GM.1011	FUEL LIFT PUMP KIT	1
252GM.1007	AC FUEL PUMP	1
250GM.1119	FUEL PIPE	1
252GM.1009	PUSH ROD	1
252GM.1010	BANJO BOLT	1
250GM.1120	BANJO UNION	1
250GM.1122	COPPER WASHER	1
LIST 73B	FUEL SOLENOID	1
402GM.152	STARTER MOTOR	1

RN TYPE ALTERNATORS

FRAME RN 4050 – 4KVA

Armature	209750–1	(1 per alternator)
Set Field Coils	260138–1	(1 per alternator)
Brush Holder	863DDE37	(4 per alternator)
Brush Grade M70	6.3mm x 8mm x 16mm	(8 per alternator)
Voltage Regulator	ES/120	(1 per alternator)

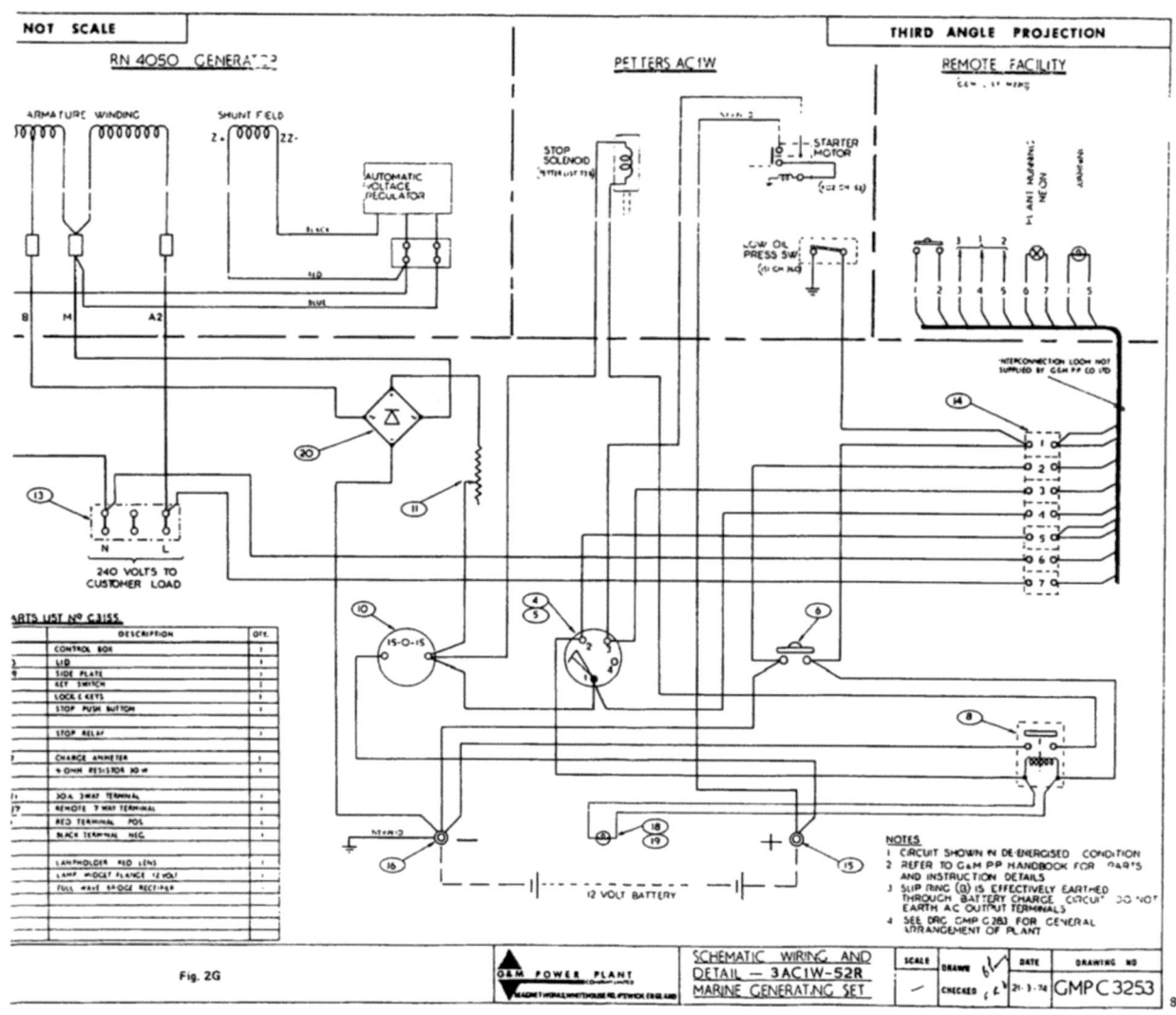

Fig. 2G — Schematic Wiring and Detail — 3AC1W-52R Marine Generating Set — Drawing No. GMPC 3253

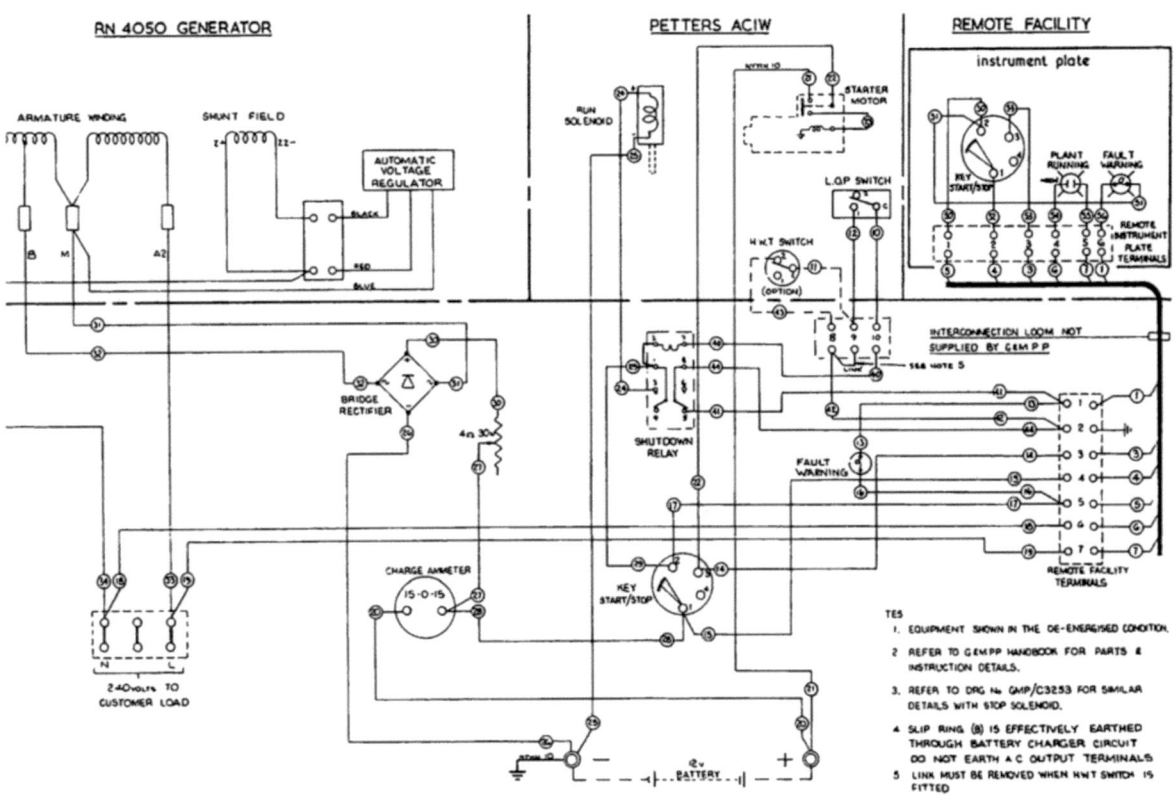

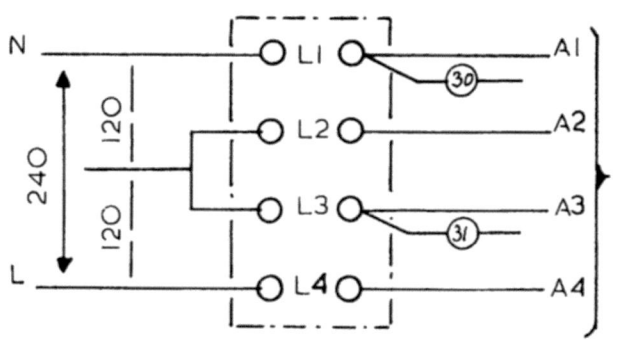

SECTION H
SC 21 ALTERNATOR

1	Introduction
2	Voltage Regulati
3	Maintenance
4	Rotor Removal
5	Fault Finding

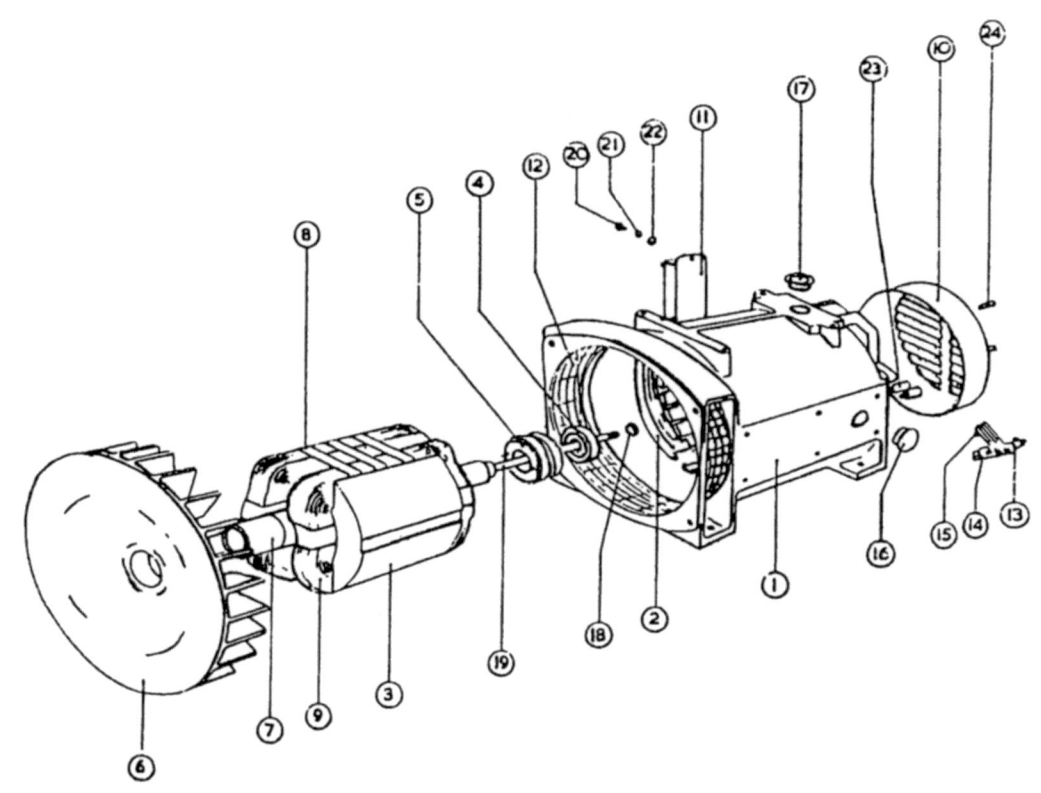

KEY TO GENERATOR PARTS

1. Frame
2. Stator core c/w windings
3. Rotor core
4. Bearing non drive end
5. Slipring
6. Fan
7. Shaft
8. Winding retaining clip
9. Winding – rotor
10. Endcover
11. A.V.R.
12. Screen
13. Brush arm stud and insulati
14. Brush holder
15. Brush
16. Blind grommet
17. Grommet
18. Self locking nut
19. Shaft stud
20. A.V.R. fixing screw
21. A.V.R. fixing lock washer
22. A.V.R. fixing plain washer
23. Suppressor
24. End cover fixing screw

1 INTRODUCTION

This machine has been specially developed to meet the demand for a lightweight engine driven rapid-response two pole generator. Self-excited and automatic voltage regulator controlled, it is of compact drip-proof rotating field construction with a total absence of complication. It comprises essentially only a wound stator core, a salient pole rotating field system and a solid state automatic voltage regulator, all contained in a die cast aluminium frame.

2 Voltage Regulation

Voltage regulation is ± 2½% from cold to hot and inclusive of a power factor range of 0.8 lagging to unity and of normal engine speed variations.

Adjustment

(a) Remove the generator end cover to expose the A.V.R. which is mounted on the right hand side.

(b) Remove the cap on the A.V.R. to gain access to the voltage adjusting screw.

(c) Using a screwdriver Figure 1.
Turn CLOCKWISE to INCREASE the volts
Turn ANTICLOCKWISE to DECREASE the volts.

(d) Adjust in small steps and do not exceed the maximum voltage of the generator.

FIGURE 1

NOTE:—

It is important that the generator is run at the correct speed while setting up the voltage. The A.V.R. is fitted with an underspeed protection circuit which is a safety circuit to prevent damage to the rotor occurring at low speed. This circuit reduces the output voltage approximately proportional to speed.

3 Maintenance

(a) The bearings are of the sealed for life type and require no maintenance other than being replaced at the end of their life. Bearing life will vary according to the type of drive and machine loading, but would normally be expected to be about 10,000 hours.

(b) Inspect the brushes and sliprings every 500 hours. Replace the brushes when they are worn to within 3 mm of the brush holder at the centre. Hold up the arm of the brush holder and remove the worn brush. The new brush should be pushed firmly into position in the arm and it should be bedded using a medium grade abrasive cloth. If the sliprings are pitted or badly marked, the rotor should be removed and the sliprings lightly skimmed.

(c) The generator must be periodically inspected and any accumulation of dirt or oil must be removed. Air inlet and outlet openings must be kept unobstructed.

(d) Inspect all wiring connections for tightness.

(e) Check that all screws and studs are tight.

4 Rotor Removal

(a) Remove the generator end cover.

(b) Prop up the brushes using a piece of stiff material approximately 60mm x 38mm between the brushes Figure 2.

(c) Unscrew the four 8mm nuts securing the generator frame to the flange adaptor/drive end bracket.

(d) Remove the generator holding down bolts.

(e) The generator frame should now be removed leaving the rotor mounted on the engine shaft or the rotor should be withdrawn from the generator frame in the case of a two bearing type.

(f) Unscrew the self locking nut from the shaft stud.

(g) The rotor shaft should now be released from the engine tapered shaft. This is achieved by supporting the rotor in one hand and with a hide mallet strike firmly on one of the pole faces.

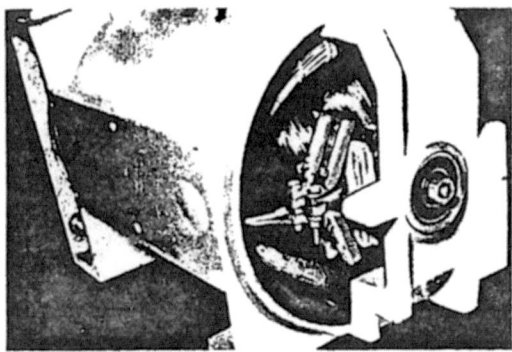

FIGURE 2

NOTE:—

Loss of residual voltage may occur when the rotor is removed from the stator. In this event it can be restored as set out in section 5.

5 Fault Finding

Before assuming a generator fault, checks should be made to establish that the apparatus and cables connecting it to the generator are sound. Also any fuses, switches or circuit breakers should be checked.

(a) Check all internal connections for tightness.

(b) Inspect the brushes and sliprings ensuring that the brushes are in firm contact with the sliprings.

(c) Check that the external linking arrangement and any other connections are correctly made. If there is any doubt concerning a switch, the leads to it should be removed and temporarily joined together.

Residual Voltage

Remove the A.V.R. leads L1 and L2. With the generator running at its correct speed, measure the residual voltage across leads A1 and A2. This should be at least 4 volts.

NOTE

Residual voltage is the voltage generated in the stator winding due to the small amount of magnetism retained in the rotor iron circuit when the excitation current ceases to flow. Residual voltage is necessary to cause self-excitation.

If this voltage is less than 4 volts it must be increased by restoring the residual magnetism. This is achieved by disconnecting the field leads X and XX from the AVR and applying for about 3 seconds a 12 volt D.C. supply to leads X and XX.

86

NOTE:—

Lead X is positive

Before re-connecting the AVR the generator must be stopped.

Separate Excitation

(a) Disconnect leads X and XX from the AVR.

(b) Connect a 12 volt D.C. supply to leads X and XX (Lead X is positive)

(c) Measure the voltage of each section of the stator windings ie. A1—A2 and A3—A4. If the generator windings are connected in parallel, they must be separated for this test. The voltage should be the same for each section. Any marked difference indicates a faulty stator winding.

(d) Run the generator at its correct speed.

(e) No voltage or only residual voltage across each section indicates an open circuit somewhere in the field circuit and this would be confirmed by the absence of a small inductive spark when disconnecting the supply. Check leads X and XX and brush contact before assuming the fault is in the rotor.

NOTE:—

Care should be taken when disconnecting the supply as a high voltage is generated in the field coil as the magnetic field collapses.

(f) If the voltage in each section is close to the nominal value this indicates a fault in the A.V.R.

Rotor Resistance Check

(a) Remove leads X and XX from the brush holders.

(b) With a suitable instrument, measure the resistance of the rotor winding, connecting the instrument leads to the terminal posts on the sliprings. The value obtained should be within 5% of that tabulated below.

NOTE:—

The figures quoted are correct only at 16.5°C and vary approximately 10% for a 25°C change in temperature.

(c) When replacing the brush leads X is positive and should be fitted to the brush holder nearest the bearing.

Rotor Resistance (ohms) (all machines)	Stator Resistance		No-load Excitation	
	50Hz machines	60Hz machines	amps	volts (cold)
11.1	1.03	0.67	0.85	10.5

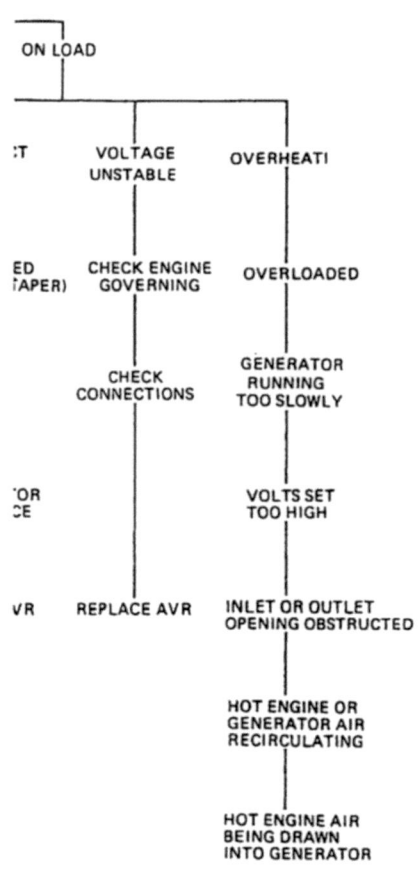

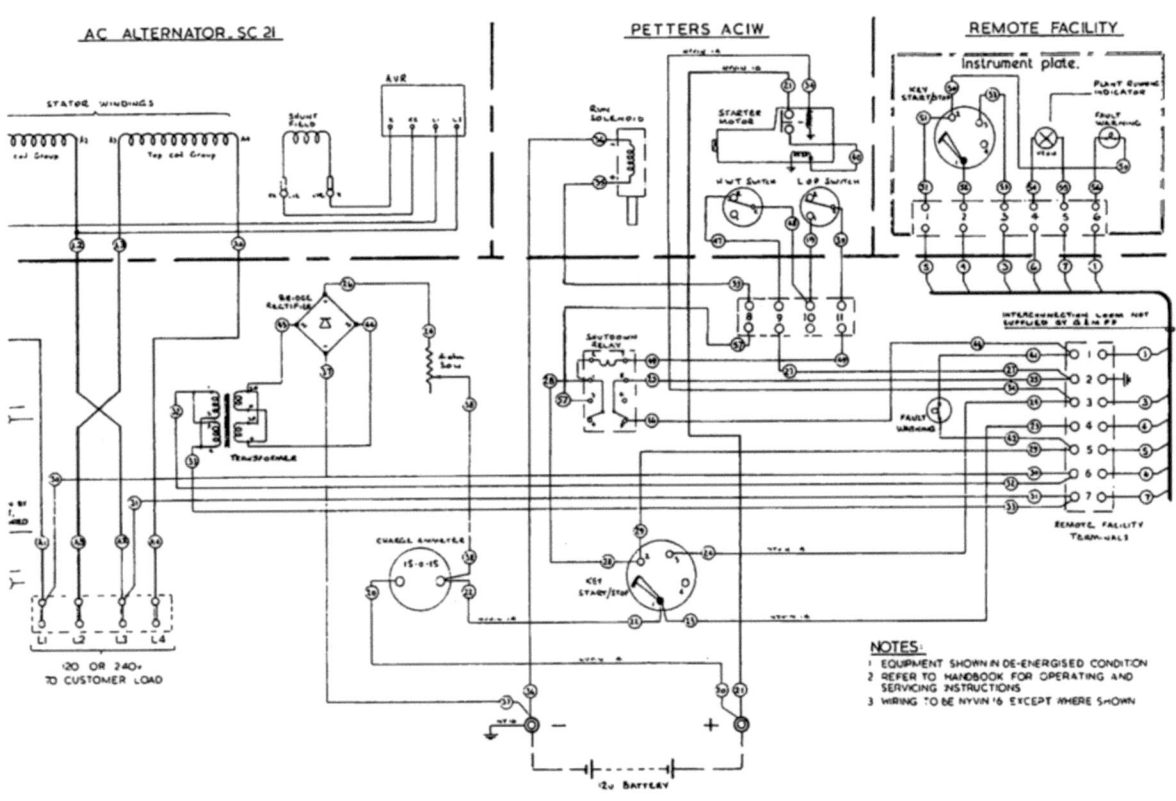

GM Marine Diesel

Lister-Petter Series AC1W Dieselite Marine Engine

Operating and Workshop Manual